Microsoft

OneNote 2013 Plain & Simple

Peter Weverka

Published with the authorization of Microsoft Corporation by:
O'Reilly Media, Inc.
1005 Gravenstein Highway North
Sebastopol, California 95472

ISBN: 978-0-7356-6934-5

1 2 3 4 5 6 7 8 9 TI 8 7 6 5 4 3

Printed and bound in Canada

Microsoft Press books are available through booksellers and distributors worldwide. If you need support related to this book, email Microsoft Press Book Support at *mspinput@microsoft.com*. Please tell us what you think of this book at *http://www.microsoft.com/learning/booksurvey*.

Acquisitions Editor: Kenyon Brown
Developmental Editor: Jennifer Fulton
Production Editor: Kristen Borg
Editorial Production: Peter Amirault
Technical Reviewer: Ben Schorr
Copyeditor: Bob Russell
Indexer: Angela Howard
Cover Design: Twist Creative • Seattle
Cover Composition: Zyg Group, LLC
Illustrator: S4Carlisle Publishing Services

For Al Smithee

Contents

Storing your notes. **39**

Writing basic notes **55**

5 Taking notes to another level **75**

6 Putting a table in a note **99**

Acknowledgments

Thanks to Ken Brown of O'Reilly Media for giving me the opportunity to write this book, to Jennifer Fulton for suggesting how to improve it, and to Ben Schorr for making sure that all the instructions are indeed accurate. Thanks as well to the O'Reilly team for their excellent layout work.

About this book

1

Microsoft OneNote 2013 Plain & Simple is for users of Microsoft OneNote 2013 who want to make the most of the program and learn how to do tasks quickly. Don't look in this book to find out how OneNote 2013 works. Instead, look in this book to find out how *you* can get *your* work done faster and better by using OneNote.

You can use this book as a tutorial or a reference. Read it one section at a time to become an expert on OneNote or keep it by your computer to refer to it when you need help. This book was written and designed so that you can get the information you need and complete tasks right away.

In this section:

- No computerese!
- The path of least resistance
- A quick overview
- A few assumptions
- What's new in OneNote 2013
- Adapting task procedures for touchscreens
- A final word

No computerese!

This book scrupulously avoids computerese, computerspeak, and nerd-talk. You will not scratch your head or grimace over computer jargon as you read this book.

For each task, you get a quick overview and the background information you need to proceed wisely. Then, you plunge right in. You get concise, step-by-step instructions for completing the task. And each set of instructions is accompanied by screenshots that show you precisely how to do the task and where to do it in OneNote.

Occasionally, you encounter a "See Also" element that refers you to a task similar to the one being described. You also find "Tips" that offer shortcuts and other useful advice. When you need to tread softly or carefully, you find a "Caution" element explaining why caution is the order of the day.

The path of least resistance

More often than not, you can accomplish the same task in OneNote 2013 by using different methods. For example, you can create a table with the Insert Table dialog box or the Table drop-down menu.

Because there aren't enough pages in this book to cover all the ways to complete each task, I sometimes cover the easiest way only. In this book, if I can't be comprehensive and describe every technique, I choose the path of least resistance—the one that is easiest for you to follow.

A quick overview

This book is your guide to getting the most from OneNote. It's jam-packed with how-to's, advice, shortcuts, and tips. Here is a bare outline of what you'll find:

Sections 2 and 3 get you up and running. They explain the basics of creating, opening, and navigating notebooks. They also show you how to create the sections, section groups, pages, and page groups you need to organize and store notes.

Section 4 explains the nitty-gritty of OneNote: how to write a note; format, move, and copy text; and create bulleted and numbered lists.

Section 5 describes advanced note-taking, including how to write outlines, insert pictures and screen clippings in notes, attach a file and file printout to a note, write math equations, and take audio and video notes. You also find out how to jot down a quick note and place it later on into a notebook.

Section 6 explains all you need to know about formatting and laying out tables, including how to create an Excel spreadsheet in a note and how to convert a OneNote table into an Excel spreadsheet.

Section 7 is all about linking. It explores how to create links between different notebooks, sections, and pages; how to hyperlink to webpages and files; and how to take linked notes.

Section 8 describes all the things that you can do to make working with OneNote easier, including how to minimize the ribbon, Notebooks pane, and page tabs; how to dock OneNote; and how to change screen views.

Section 9 takes on the spelling checker, including how to check the spelling of foreign text. Section 10 explains how to draw notes with lines, free-form lines, and shapes. Section 11 describes tagging and other ways to organize notes, such as moving and copying. Section 12 explores how to search for stray notes.

Section 13 explains housecleaning chores, including how to delete and restore sections and pages and how to back up a notebook. Section 14 shows how to use the Research pane to investigate topics and translate foreign-language text.

Section 15 looks at distributing notes by printing them as well as sending them by email, and how to save OneNote pages, sections, and notebooks in alternate file formats. Section 16 explores how to use OneNote and Microsoft Outlook 2013 to handle tasks, calendar events, meetings, and contact information.

Section 17 describes how to share notebooks and how to find and read notes written by your coauthors. Section 18 explains how to customize the ribbon and the Quick Access Toolbar to make yourself a more efficient user of OneNote.

Section 19 delves into OneNote Web App, the online version of OneNote, and how you can use it to collaborate with others when taking notes.

A few assumptions

Pardon me, but I made a few assumptions about you, the reader of this book.

I assumed that you are experienced enough with computers to know the basics: how to turn the thing on and what "click" and "double-click" mean, for example. I assumed that Microsoft Office 2013 (OneNote is part of the Office 2013 suite) is already installed on your computer.

> ⚠ **CAUTION** This book also assumes that you are using OneNote 2013, which is part of Office 2013. There is another version of OneNote, OneNote App for Windows 8, which is available through the Windows Store. This version is optimized for touch-enabled devices, and it looks very different from the one described in this book. Although you can perform most of the tasks in this book by using OneNote App for Windows 8, the steps are slightly different. To learn more about OneNote App for Windows 8, see the book, *Microsoft Office Professional 2013 for Touch Devices*, by Katherine Murray.

What's new in OneNote 2013

With each edition of OneNote, the makers of the application endeavor to improve it and add new features. OneNote 2013 is no different. Following is a rundown of new features in OneNote 2013.

Starting OneNote in Windows 8

If your computer runs Windows 8, the procedure for starting OneNote is probably new to you. To start OneNote, click the OneNote 2013 tile on the Apps screen. The application opens on the Windows desktop.

Follow these steps to start OneNote from the Apps screen:

1 Right-click the Start screen to display the Windows taskbar.

2 Click All Apps.

(continued on next page)

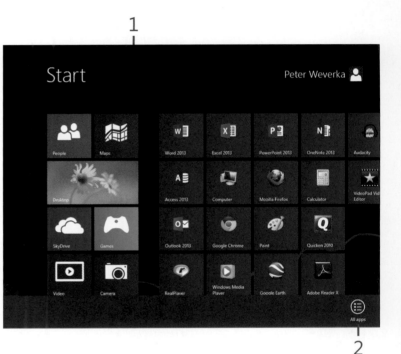

Starting OneNote in Windows 8 *(continued)*

3 Scroll to the right side of the Apps screen.

4 Click the OneNote 2013 tile.

⚠

CAUTION   You might have installed another version of OneNote from the Windows Store—OneNote App for Windows 8. If so, it appears in the Apps list as simply OneNote. The version of OneNote described in this book appears grouped together with the other Microsoft Office 2013 apps tiles, with the name OneNote 2013. Make sure you click the OneNote 2013 tile to start the program.

Starting OneNote in Windows 7

If your computer runs Windows 7, follow these steps to start OneNote:

1 Click the Start button.

2 Click All Programs.

3 Click Microsoft Office 2013.

4 Click OneNote 2013.

1 2

3

4

Navigating the Backstage view

To visit the Backstage view, on the ribbon, click the File tab. The Backstage view offers commands for creating, opening, printing, sharing, exporting, and sending OneNote notebooks. Click a tab on the left side of the Backstage view window and you see options on the right for performing different tasks. For example, click Info and you see information about the currently open notebook.

What is different about the Backstage view in OneNote 2013 is this: it now offers a convenient Back button. You can click this button to return to the OneNote screen.

Clicking the Options tab opens the OneNote Options dialog box, in which you choose settings to make OneNote work your way.

Click the Back button to return to the OneNote screen

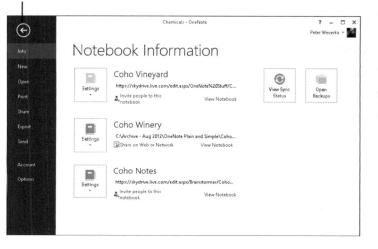

Sharing notebooks

OneNote 2013 is optimized for sharing notebooks through SkyDrive. SkyDrive is an online cloud service from Microsoft for storing and sharing files. To use SkyDrive, you must sign up for a Microsoft Account. After signing up, you can store OneNote notebooks on SkyDrive so that you can access them from anywhere—through OneNote, OneNote Mobile, or a web browser (using OneNote Web App). You can also share notebooks stored on SkyDrive with your friends and colleagues when you need to work collaboratively.

You can also share notebooks through a SharePoint site, a company network, or Microsoft Office 365 (which provides a SharePoint site or SkyDrive for file collaboration). SharePoint is used by companies to share files. It provides a structured method for collaboration through blogs, wikis, and company news updates. To share notebooks through SharePoint, save the notebook to a folder on the SharePoint site. To share notebooks through a company network, save the notebook in a shared folder.

Office 365 is a subscription service that provides online storage of notebooks and other services. Depending on your subscription level, you can share notebooks through SkyDrive or through a SharePoint team site designed for collaboration.

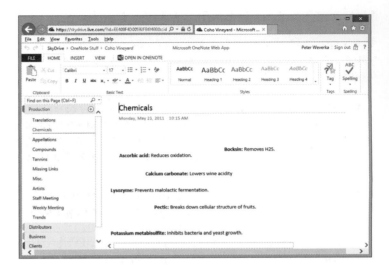

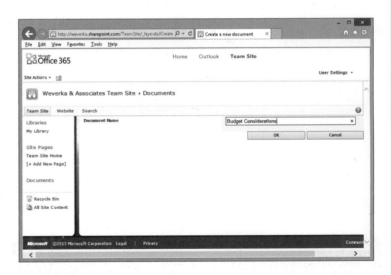

SEE ALSO To learn how to share notebooks through SkyDrive or SharePoint, read "Sharing a notebook" on page 226.

SEE ALSO To learn how to create and share notebooks on Office 365, read "Creating a notebook in Office 365" on page 260.

TIP You can sign up for a Microsoft Account at *https://signup. live.com*. After creating an account, you can log on to SkyDrive and access your files and OneNote Web App at *www.skydrive.com*.

Using the Send To OneNote tool

The Send To OneNote tool opens in its own window when you start OneNote. It offers a convenient way to access three OneNote commands:

Take a screen clipping · Send a file to OneNote · Write a quick note

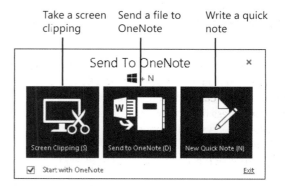

- **Screen Clipping**   Click Screen Clipping in the window to capture part of an open window on your computer screen as a screenshot. (You can also take a screen clipping on the Insert tab by clicking the Screen Clipping button.)

- **Send To OneNote**   Click Send To OneNote to copy a Microsoft Word document, Microsoft Excel spreadsheet, or Microsoft PowerPoint presentation to a page in a notebook. Before clicking Send To OneNote, open the document, spreadsheet, or presentation.

- **New Quick Note**   Click New Quick Note in the window to write a quick note—a note that you can move later to a page. Quick Notes are stored temporarily in the Quick Notes folder until you move them elsewhere.

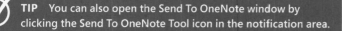 **TIP**   If you prefer the Send To OneNote Tool *not* to appear when you start OneNote, clear the Start With OneNote check box located at the bottom of the Send To OneNote window.

 TIP   You can also open the Send To OneNote window by clicking the Send To OneNote Tool icon in the notification area.

 SEE ALSO   To learn all the details of taking screen clippings, read "Taking a screen clipping" on page 92.

SEE ALSO   To learn the details of sending files to OneNote with the Send To OneNote command, read "Sending files to OneNote" on page 86.

SEE ALSO   To learn all the details of writing quick notes, read "Writing quick notes" on page 76.

Updating your Office account

Office is available in two basic versions: Office 2013 and Office 365. Office 2013 is standard "boxed" software. It comes in different editions—Office Home and Student or Office Home and Business—that might or might not include Microsoft Outlook, Microsoft Publisher, and Microsoft Access.

Office 365, on the other hand, is a subscription service that provides various services (depending on your subscription level), such as cloud storage, email, shared calendars, instant messaging, online editing of Office documents (using Office Web App and/or streaming versions of the full programs—Office on Demand), public website, and a team site for document collaboration.

If you subscribe to Office 365 Home Premium or an Office 365 service that supplies Office, OneNote and your other Office programs are updated automatically during your subscription period.

If you purchase Office 2013 as a classic software package, without the subscription and without the services, you will receive updates during the entire product cycle (approximately two years or so), as well. These updates will also install automatically, provided you've instructed Windows to do that. Display the Windows desktop by clicking the Desktop tile on the Start screen. Move the mouse pointer to the lower-right corner of the screen and click the Settings charm. Click Control Panel, click Systems And Security, click Windows Update, and then click Change Settings. In the Change Settings dialog box that opens, select the Give Me Updates For Other Microsoft Products When I Update Windows check box and click OK.

In the Account window in OneNote, you can view the list of services to which you are connected—SkyDrive, Office 365 SharePoint site, and others. To open the Account window, click File to display the Backstage view and then click the Account tab.

By clicking the About OneNote button in the Account window, you can open a dialog box that displays your Product ID number.

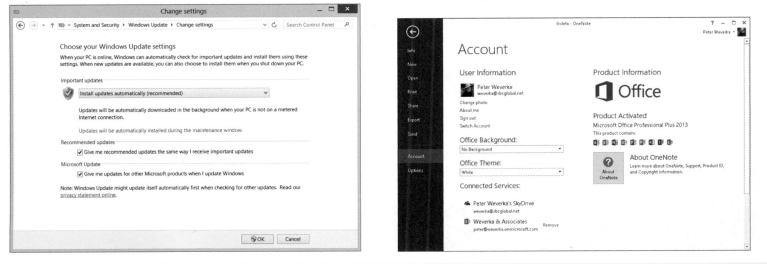

Sorting table data

Sorting means to rearrange the information in a list or table in alphabetical or numerical order. In a table of names, for example, sorting the list in alphabetical order from A to Z makes finding a name easier. In a table of numbers, sorting the table in numerical order makes comparing the numbers easier.

With the Sort command, you can sort a table in ascending or descending order and make your table easier to understand.

Click the Sort button to sort table data

SEE ALSO To learn the ins and outs of sorting information in a table, read "Sorting data in a table" on page 105.

Converting tables to Excel spreadsheets

OneNote tables are nice indeed, but they don't offer all the tools for analyzing data that you find in Excel. If you want to perform data analyses on the information in a OneNote table, consider converting your table to an Excel spreadsheet.

OneNote offers the Convert To Excel Spreadsheet command for doing just that.

After a table is converted, you can click its Edit button to display Excel tools for editing, formatting, sorting, and analyzing table data.

Click Convert To Excel Spreadsheet to turn a table into a spreadsheet

SEE ALSO To learn how to edit an embedded Excel spreadsheet in OneNote, read "Edit an Excel spreadsheet in a note" on page 111.

Generating Excel spreadsheets in a OneNote note

If you know that you will need to crunch the numbers in the notes that you write, create an Excel spreadsheet in a note before you enter the numbers. This way, you can take advantage of all the Excel features and commands for analyzing data as you enter it.

The Spreadsheet button offers an option to create an Excel spreadsheet right inside OneNote.

Click the Edit button in the embedded spreadsheet to access Excel tools for editing, formatting, sorting, and analyzing data.

Choose New Excel Spreadsheet to create a spreadsheet in OneNote

SEE ALSO To learn how to create spreadsheets in OneNote, read "Creating an Excel spreadsheet in a note" on page 109.

Inserting pictures from online sources

Pictures are great for illustrating ideas, and OneNote makes it easy to obtain pictures for notes. With the Online Pictures command, you can obtain pictures from Office.com, the Internet, a SkyDrive folder, or Flickr.com.

Enter a search term to search for pictures at Office.com

SEE ALSO To learn how to search for pictures online and insert pictures in notes, read "Inserting a picture from an Internet source" on page 90.

Choosing a page template

When you need a new page, you can create it by using a template—a page designed for a specific purpose, such as taking meeting notes or creating a to-do list. Although page templates are not new to OneNote 2013, they are certainly easier to use.

As well as choosing a template from OneNote, you can create a template of your own and use it to create as many new pages as you want.

Choose a template for a page in the Templates task pane.

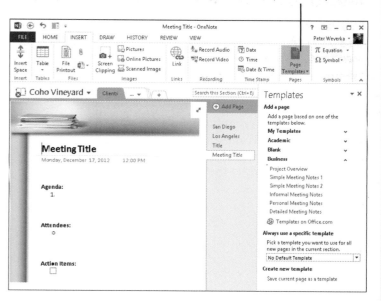

SEE ALSO To learn how to choose a template when creating a page, read "Creating pages" on page 43.

SEE ALSO To learn how to create a template, read "Creating and managing templates" on page 45.

Using the Thesaurus to better express your ideas

Rather than scratch your head when you can't find the right word, you can give the Thesaurus a try. Although the Thesaurus existed in previous versions of OneNote, it wasn't easy to locate and use.

The Thesaurus lists synonyms of a word you choose in a note. If one of the synonyms expresses your ideas better, you can insert it in a note in place of the word you chose. You can also search for words in the Thesaurus pane.

Search for synonyms in the Thesaurus pane

SEE ALSO   To find out whether the Thesaurus works for you, read "Finding the right word by using the Thesaurus" on page 203.

Adapting task procedures for touchscreens

In this book, I provide instructions based on traditional keyboard and mouse input methods. If you're using OneNote on a touch-enabled device, you might be giving commands by tapping with your finger or with a stylus. If so, substitute a tapping action any time I instruct you to click a user interface element. Also note that when I tell you to enter information in OneNote, you can do so by typing on a keyboard, tapping in the entry text field under discussion to display and use the On-Screen Keyboard, or even speaking aloud, depending on how your computer is set up and your personal preferences.

A final word

I hope you find this book helpful. When I wrote it, I had these goals in mind:

- To provide clear instructions for completing OneNote tasks

- To steer you to things you can do in OneNote that you didn't know you could do

- To make you a confident OneNote user

Good luck in your adventures with OneNote!

Getting started with OneNote 2013

Your first task in Microsoft OneNote 2013 is to create a notebook for storing the notes you write. After you create a notebook, you create sections for storing the pages where notes are written, pages for storing notes, and then the notes themselves.

In OneNote 2013, notes are stored in a notebook-section-pages hierarchy that is designed to help you categorize information, write notes, and retrieve notes. Navigating in OneNote is a matter of using the Notebooks pane, section tabs, and page tabs to go from place to place. In the Notebooks pane, where notebook names are listed, you can collapse and expand notebooks to hide or display their sections.

You can open notebooks to work on them, close them when you no longer need them, and rename them as needed.

If you used Microsoft OneNote 2007, be sure to convert your 2007 notebooks to 2010-2013 notebooks. OneNote offers a special command for doing that.

In this section:

- What's where in OneNote 2013
- Using the ribbon
- Using the Quick Access Toolbar
- Taking advantage of the notebook-section-pages hierarchy
- Creating a notebook
- Renaming a notebook
- Opening a notebook
- Closing a notebook
- Collapsing and expanding notebooks in the Notebooks pane
- Navigating in OneNote
- Converting OneNote 2007 notebooks to 2010-2013 and back again

What's where in OneNote 2013

The purpose of OneNote is to make it easier for you to record, store, organize, and find notes. To that end, the OneNote screen is divided into these areas:

- **Notebooks pane**   Lists the names of open notebooks. Below each notebook name are the names of its sections and section groups. Click a section name to open a different section in any open notebook.

- **Section tabs**   Shows the names of sections, with the name of each section on its own tab. Section groups appear to the right of the section tabs. Click a tab to go to a different section. Click a section group button to display its sections.

- **Page tabs**   Lists the names of pages and subpages in the currently open section. Pages are stored in sections. Click a page tab to open a different page.

- **Page**   Shows the notes and other items on the current page.

The Notebooks pane   Section tabs   Section group button   Page tabs

> **(→) TRY THIS**   Click a section name in the Notebooks pane and notice that a new section opens. Then, click a section tab. You can open a different section by clicking a section name in the Notebooks pane or the section tabs

> **(🔍) SEE ALSO**   To learn how to expand and collapse the Notebooks pane and page tabs, read "Collapsing and expanding the Notebooks pane and page tabs" on page 128.

Using the ribbon

The ribbon initially appears as an assortment of tabs positioned along the top of the OneNote window. When you expand the ribbon by clicking a tab, it displays buttons and commands so you can perform various tasks.

There are seven tabs in all: File, Home, Insert, Draw, History, Review, and View. Clicking the File tab opens the Backstage view, where you find commands for doing file-related tasks.

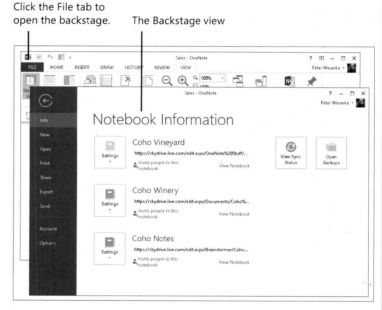

Click a tab name on the ribbon to display it and use its buttons and commands. After choosing a button or command, the ribbon automatically collapses; you see only the tabs and have more workspace on the screen. However, you can show the full ribbon all the time if you want.

The other tabs provide buttons and commands for doing similar tasks. For example, click the View tab to change your view of the OneNote screen.

Within each tab, buttons and commands are divided into groups. You can see the group names along the bottom of the ribbon. These group names help you to understand what buttons and commands do.

Besides the standard tabs, OneNote sometimes presents a *contextual tab*. Contextual tabs appear on the ribbon only when you need them. For example, when you work on a table, the Table Tools | Layout tab appears; it offers commands for working with tables. Look for contextual tabs to the right of the standard tabs on the ribbon.

SEE ALSO To learn all the different ways to hide and display the ribbon, read "Showing and collapsing the ribbon" on page 131.

TIP Move the pointer over a button or command on the ribbon to see a ScreenTip that briefly describes what the button or command does. If a shortcut key combination (for example, Ctrl+B) is available for activating a command, it appears in the ScreenTip.

Using the Quick Access Toolbar

Quick Access toolbar

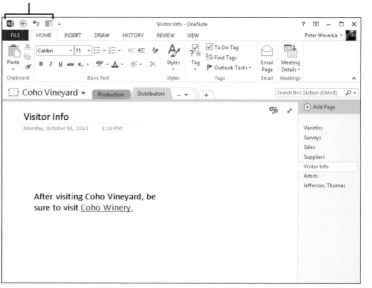

Above the ribbon, in the upper-left corner of the window, is the Quick Access Toolbar. This toolbar offers three convenient buttons: Back, Undo, and Dock To Desktop. On tablets, the Quick Access Toolbar offers a fourth button: Touch/Mouse Mode.

What's more, you can add and remove buttons from the Quick Access Toolbar. You can even place it below the ribbon.

> **SEE ALSO** To learn how to add or remove buttons on the Quick Access Toolbar, read "Adding or removing Quick Access Toolbar buttons" on page 234.

> **SEE ALSO** To learn how to move the Quick Access Toolbar below the ribbon, read "Repositioning the Quick Access Toolbar" on page 237.

Taking advantage of the notebook-section-pages hierarchy

In OneNote 2013, notes are stored in a notebook-section-pages hierarchy, with the highest-level unit of storage being the notebook. Within each notebook, you create sections, and within sections, you create pages.

How you organize information in this hierarchy is important not only for retrieving information but also for conceptualizing it. In For academic work, for example, you can create one notebook for the class, one section for each lecture, and within each section, a page for each subject in the lecture. When the time comes to study for the final examination, you will know where to retrieve information about each subject, and moreover, your notebook-sections-pages structure will help you to get a sense of how the subjects fit together.

The goal is to create notebooks, sections, and pages so that information is stored in a meaningful fashion that makes retrieving information easier. As part of that goal, think of descriptive names for each of these elements when you create them.

From largest to smallest, OneNote offers these units for storing notes:

- **Notebook**   The place where all information is stored. The names of open notebooks appear in the Notebooks pane.

- **Section**   A subcategory of a notebook, used to store pages. The names of sections in a notebook appear on the Notebooks pane below the notebook's name as well as on the section tabs.

- **Section groups**   A means of organizing sections. You can store sections in a section group and, in so doing, be able to find and manage them more easily. After you select a section group in the section tabs, only the sections in the group appear in the section tabs.

- **Page and subpage**   The place where notes are recorded. Pages and subpages are stored in sections. The names of pages and subpages in the currently open section appear in the page tabs on the right side of the screen; names on subpage tabs are indented.

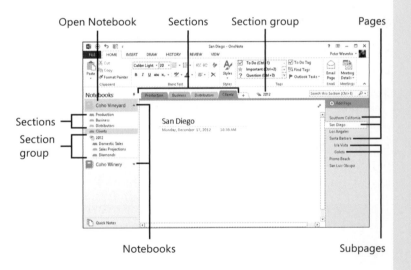

Creating a notebook

OneNote 2013 is unusual in that you choose a folder for storing a notebook when you create it. In most applications, you create the file first and then choose a storage folder when you save the file for the first time. In OneNote, however, there isn't a Save button or Save command; notes are saved as soon as you write them.

The first time you start OneNote, the application prompts you to create a sample notebook called Personal Notebook. From that point forward, when you open OneNote, the previous notebook(s) you were working on open.

You can create a new notebook on your local computer, network, SkyDrive, or SharePoint. OneNote creates a new folder when you create a notebook. This folder is named after the notebook itself. For example, if you named the notebook "Research," the folder is named "Research." Sections that you create for your notebook are stored in the folder in the form of OneNote section files.

Create a notebook

1 Click the File tab to display the Backstage view.

2 Click the New tab.

3 Choose Computer to store your notebook on your computer or another option to store it elsewhere, such as SharePoint or SkyDrive.

4 In the Notebook Name text box, enter a descriptive name for your notebook.

5 Click the Create In A Different Folder link.

(continued on next page)

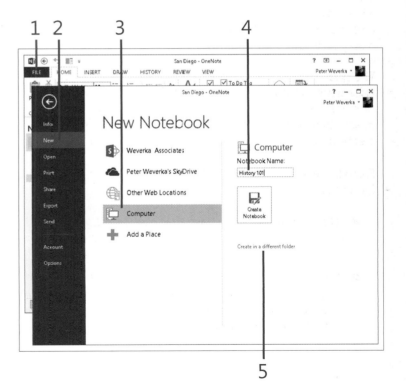

Create a notebook *(continued)*

6 In the Create New Notebook dialog box, select the folder where you want to store your new notebook, and then click Create.

7 Click Create Notebook.

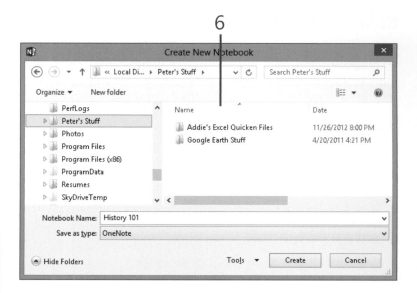

> ⚠ **CAUTION** OneNote creates a section and page for a notebook when you create it. The section is called "New Section 1," and the page is called "Untitled Page." Be sure to enter names of your own for the section and page in your new notebook.

> → **TIP** By default, notebooks are stored in the default notebook location. To find out where this location is, on the ribbon, click File and then click the Options tab. Then, in the OneNote Options dialog box, select the Save & Backup category. Under Save, you can see the default notebook location. To change this location, select Default Notebook Location, click the Modify button, and then, in the Select Folder dialog box, select a folder.

> 🔍 **SEE ALSO** To learn how to save a notebook on SharePoint or SkyDrive, see "Sharing a notebook" on page 226.

> → **TRY THIS** Look for a Save button in OneNote. You won't find it! OneNote saves data as soon as you enter it, and you don't have to click a Save button.

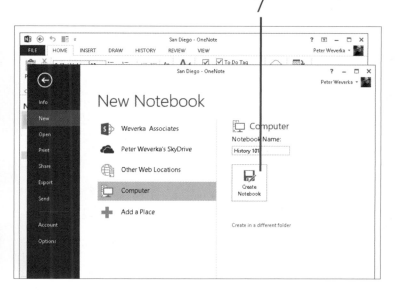

Renaming a notebook

You can rename a OneNote 2013 notebook if the original name no longer serves your purposes. Changing the name of a notebook might help you to better identify its contents and purpose.

Rename a notebook

1 In the Notebooks pane, right-click the name of the notebook that you want to rename.

2 On the shortcut menu that opens, click Properties.

3 In the Notebook Properties dialog box, enter a name in the Display Name text box.

4 Click OK.

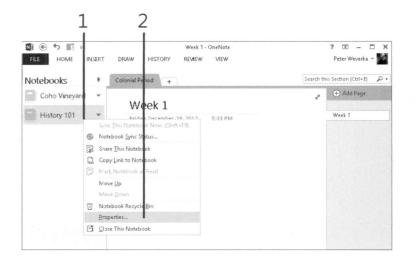

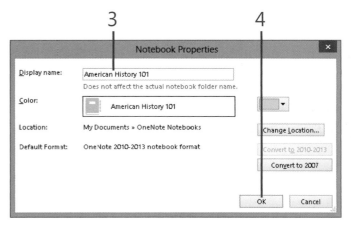

> ⚠️ **CAUTION** Renaming a notebook does not rename the folder in which it is stored. Instead, the folder retains the original name of the notebook. This name retention can be confusing if you want to open a notebook in the Open Notebook dialog box, in which your notebook's folder is listed under the notebook's original name, not the new name you gave it.

> ➔ **TIP** While the Notebook Properties dialog box is open, you can choose a color for your new notebook by clicking the drop-down arrow on the Color list box and choosing a color from the list that appears. The color appears on the notebook icon next to the notebook's name in the Notebooks pane.

Opening a notebook

You can open more than one OneNote 2013 notebook and switch between them as you work. The names of open notebooks appear the Notebooks pane.

OneNote is optimized for use with SkyDrive, so the Open Notebook window makes it easy to open notebooks stored there. You can also open notebooks that you've worked on recently or stored on your computer or on SharePoint.

Open a notebook on SkyDrive

1 Click the File tab to display the Backstage view.

2 Click the Open tab.

3 Click a notebook in the Open From SkyDrive section. (Notebooks that are already open appear with an open book icon.)

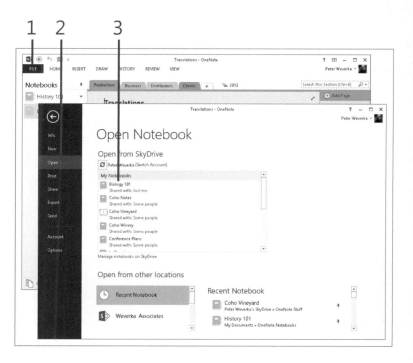

Open a notebook on your computer or on SharePoint

1 Click the File tab to display the Backstage view.

2 Click the Open tab.

3 In the Open From Other Locations section, click Recent Notebook and look for the notebook that you want to open in the Recent Notebook list. (If the notebook you want to open is in the list, you can click its name to open it.)

4 Alternatively, in the Open From Other Locations section, click your SharePoint location and look for the notebook that you want to open in the SharePoint list. Click the notebook's name to open it.

5 Again, alternatively, in the Open From Other Locations section, click Computer to open a notebook stored on your computer.

(continued on next page)

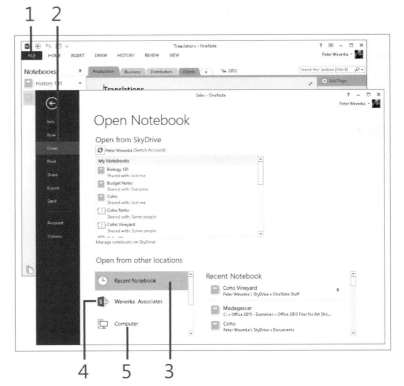

Open a notebook on your computer or on SharePoint *(continued)*

6 Open the folder in which the notebook is stored. To open the folder, either click its name in the Recent Folders list or click the Browse button (you might need to scroll down to find it) and then, in the Open Notebook dialog box, select the folder.

7 Select the Open Notebook command.

8 Click Open.

> ✓ **TIP** Notebooks in the Recent Notebook list are arranged in date order, with the notebook you opened most recently at the top of the list. To move a notebook to the top of the list, click its Pin This Item To The List button (this button appears when you hover the mouse pointer over the notebook name).

> ✓ **TIP** To open the Open Notebook dialog box without first clicking the File tab, you can either press Ctrl+O or right-click the Notebooks pane and then, on the shortcut menu that appears, click Open Notebook.

Closing a notebook

OneNote 2013 makes it pretty easy to close a notebook. You simply close it when you're through working on it. You don't have to save a notebook before closing it, because OneNote saves changes as you work.

Close a notebook

1   In the Notebooks pane, right-click the name of the notebook you want to close.

2   On the shortcut menu that appears, click Close This Notebook.

The notebook is closed and its name is removed from the Notebooks pane.

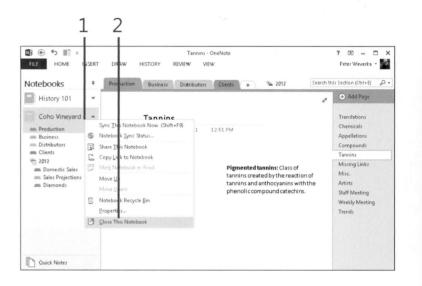

SEE ALSO   To learn how to hide and display a notebook's sections in the Notebooks pane, read "Collapsing and expanding the Notebooks pane and page tabs" on page 128.

Collapsing and expanding sections listed in the Notebooks pane

To prevent the OneNote 2013 Notebooks pane from becoming too crowded with the names of open notebooks and the names of sections in open notebooks, you can collapse a notebook.

When a notebook is collapsed, its section names don't appear in the Notebooks pane. When it is expanded, its section names reappear.

Collapse and expand sections

1 In the Notebooks pane, click the Collapse button (the up-arrow) next to a notebook name.

The section names in the notebook are hidden and the up-arrow beside the notebook name becomes a down-arrow.

2 Click the Expand button next to a notebook name to redisplay its section names.

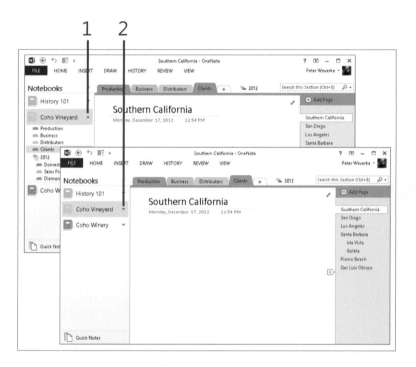

TIP You can reorder notebook names in the Notebooks pane. For example, move the notebook you use most often to the top of the list. To reorder notebook names, drag a name higher or lower on the list, or right-click a name and then, in the shortcut menu that appears, click Move Up or Move Down.

SEE ALSO To learn how to create links that you can click to quickly go to different sections and pages, read "Linking to other places in OneNote" on page 114.

Navigating in OneNote

Notes in OneNote 2013 are stored in a notebook-section-pages hierarchy. Within each notebook, you create sections, and within sections, you create pages. Getting from place to place in OneNote is a matter of using the Notebooks pane, section tabs, and page tabs.

Navigate in OneNote

1 In the Notebooks pane, click a notebook name to switch to a different notebook (if the Notebooks pane isn't open, click the Show Notebooks button).

2 In the Notebooks pane, click a section name to switch to a different section.

3 In the section tabs, click a section name to switch to a different section.

4 In the page tabs, click a page to switch to a different page.

5 Click a section group button.

   The section tabs in that section group are the only ones displayed.

6 Click the Navigate To Parent Section Group button to return to the parent sections in the notebook.

OneNote offers these keyboard shortcuts for navigating.

To go to	Press
The next or previous page in the section	Ctrl+PageDown; Ctrl+PageUp
The first or last page in the section	Alt+Home; Alt+End
The next or previous page you visited	Alt+Right Arrow; Alt+Left Arrow
The next or previous section	Ctrl+Tab; Ctrl+Shift+Tab

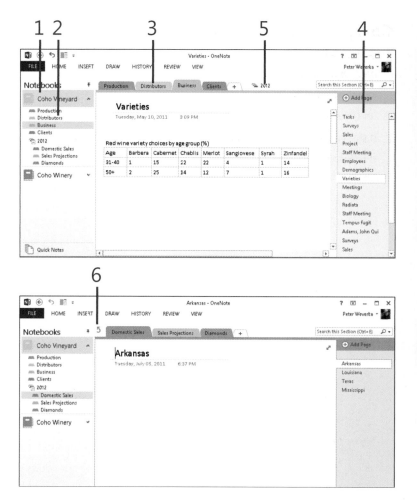

Converting OneNote 2007 notebooks to 2010–2013 and back again

You can convert Microsoft OneNote 2007 notebooks to Microsoft OneNote 2010-2013 format to take advantage of the features not available in the 2007 edition. For example, you must convert to OneNote 2010–2013 to share notebooks with the OneNote Web App.

Convert a OneNote 2007 notebook to 2010-2013

1 In the Notebooks pane, right-click the notebook that you want to convert to OneNote 2010–2013.

2 On the shortcut menu that appears, choose Properties.

3 In the Notebook Properties dialog box, click Convert To 2010-2013.

4 In the pop-up message box that appears, click OK to confirm that you want to convert the notebook.

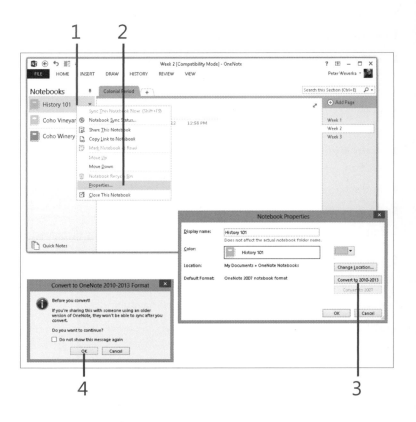

TIP When a notebook is in the 2007 format, the words "Compatibility Mode" appear next to its name in the title bar.

Convert a OneNote 2010–2013 notebook to 2007

1 In the Notebooks pane, right-click the notebook that you want to convert to OneNote 2007.

2 On the shortcut menu that appears, click Properties.

3 In the Notebook Properties dialog box, click Convert To 2007.

4 In the pop-up message box that appears, click OK to confirm that you want to convert the notebook.

Storing your notes

3

Microsoft OneNote 2013 stores notes in pages. Pages can be organized in sections, section groups, and page groups. The names of sections and section groups appear in the Notebooks pane and on the section tabs. The names of pages and subpages that make up page groups appear on the page tabs. By thoughtfully building a scheme for storing notes in sections, section groups, pages, and page groups, you can organize information meaningfully and always be able to locate information when you need it.

OneNote keeps earlier versions of pages on hand in case you want to revisit or restore an older version of a page.

And, if keeping notes private is important to you, you can password-protect a section so that only people with the password can see a section's notes.

Creating sections

Within a OneNote 2013 notebook, you can create a section for each topic that you want to address. For example, create a section for each class or staff meeting you attend. Sections are the primary means of organizing notes in a notebook.

After you create a section, a tab appears at the top of the window on which you can enter a name for the section. If you create more sections than can be displayed as tabs along the top of the window, the Show The Rest Of The Sections drop-down arrow appears; click it to display a list of the remaining sections.

When you create a new section, OneNote creates the first page in the section automatically. You can add more pages to the section as needed.

Create a section

1 Click the Create A New Section button (the plus sign in the narrow tab next to the existing section tabs). You can also press Ctrl+T.

OneNote adds a tab to the notebook.

(continued on next page)

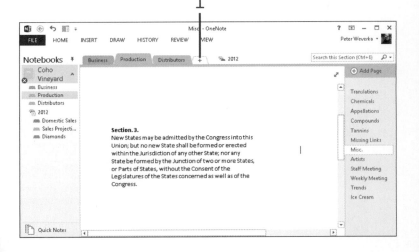

> ✓ **TIP** To rename a section, double-click its name on the section tab and type a new name.

> ✓ **TIP** To change the position of sections in the Notebooks pane or section tabs, drag the section. In the Notebooks pane, drag a section name up or down; on the section tabs, drag a section tab left or right.

Create a section *(continued)*

2 On the tab itself, type a name for the section and press Enter.

3 Type a page name.

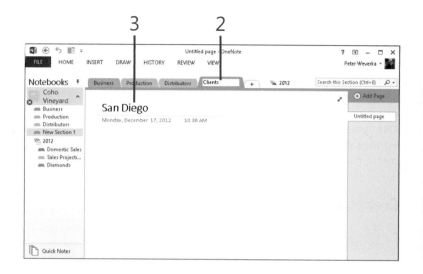

TRY THIS Each section you create is stored in a Microsoft OneNote Section (.one) file in the notebook folder where data about your notebook is kept. To see the path for this file, move the pointer over a section tab. A ScreenTip shows the path to this .one file.

SEE ALSO To learn how to move or copy a section to a different notebook, read "Moving or copying a section to another notebook" on page 162.

Creating section groups

Think of a section group as a subfolder for storing sections. You can place sections in a section group to organize similar sections together. In the Notebooks pane and section tabs, section groups always appear after sections.

After you create a section group, you can create new sections for it or move existing sections into it.

In the Notebooks pane and section tabs, section group names are marked with the section group icon, which looks like stacked folders. Section groups appear to the right of section tabs, at the top of the window. When sections/section groups cannot all be displayed, click the Show The Rest Of The Sections drop-down arrow to display a list of hidden sections/section groups.

To open a section group, click its name in the Notebooks pane or the section tabs. After you open a section group, you only see section tabs belonging to the group in the section tabs area.

Create a section group

1 Right-click a section tab.

2 On the shortcut menu that appears, click New Section Group.

A section group appears to the right of the section tabs.

3 Type a name for the section group and press Enter.

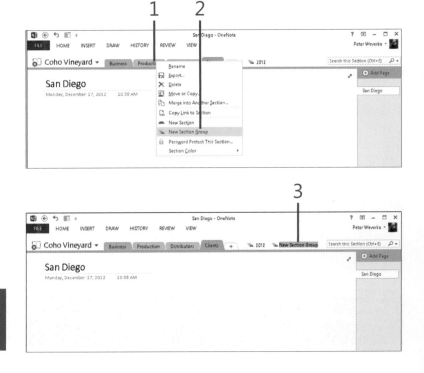

SEE ALSO To learn how to move sections into a section group, read "Moving or copying a section to another notebook" on page 162.

Creating pages

Notes are written and kept on pages. The name of the page that is currently open appears in the title bar at the top of the OneNote 2013 window, at the top of the page itself, and in the page tabs. Below its name, each page also lists the date and time that it was created.

OneNote offers templates for creating blank pages as well as pages designed for specific purposes, such as taking notes at lectures and creating to-do lists.

Create a page

1 At the top of the page tabs column, click Add Page (or press Ctrl+N).

A new page tab appears.

2 Enter a name in the page title box.

If you do not type a title for the page, the page will take on the name of the first word or phrase you enter on the page.

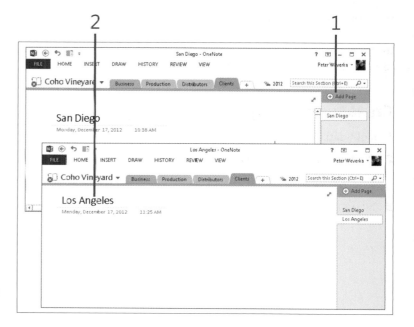

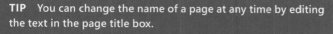 **TIP** You can change the name of a page at any time by editing the text in the page title box.

 TIP To reorder pages in a section, select a page in the pages tab and drag it up or down.

SEE ALSO To learn how to create subpages, read "Creating page groups" on page 47.

Create a page from a template

1 On the ribbon, click the Insert tab.

2 In the Pages group, click Page Templates.

3 In the Templates pane, click a templates category.

4 Click a template name.

5 Click the Close button to close the Templates pane.

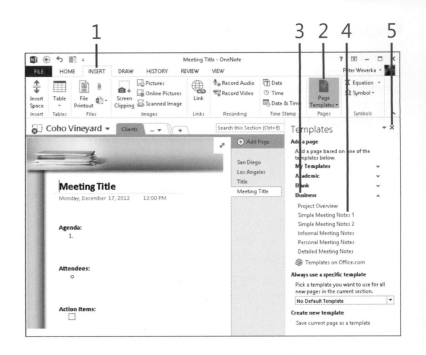

TIP You can create a page with a template you've used before without opening the Templates pane. On the Insert tab, in the Pages group, click the Page Templates arrow and then, from the menu that appears, choose one of the ten templates.

TRY THIS In the Templates pane, click the Templates At Office.com link. Your browser opens a page at Office.com where you can select from many more templates than are available in the Templates pane.

Creating and managing templates

You can create your own page templates as well as use the templates that come with OneNote 2013. In the Templates pane, templates you create are kept in the My Templates category.

To create a page template, either start with a template from OneNote and modify it or start with a blank page and format it to your liking. Then, save your page as a template.

If you don't choose a template when you create a page, pages that you create with the New Page command are made with the No Default template. However, you can choose a different template as the default page that is created automatically when you create a new page in a particular section. If you'd like, you can choose a default template for each section of your notebook.

Create a page template

1 Create a page to serve as the model for the template. On the page, include text, font, page color, and other specifications.

2 On the ribbon, click the Insert tab.

3 In the Pages group, click Page Templates.

4 In the Templates pane, click Save Current Page As A Template.

5 In the Save As Template dialog box, in the Template name text box, enter a name for the template.

6 Click Save.

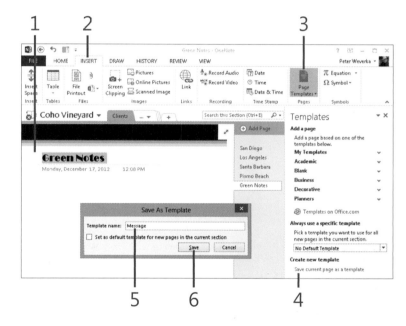

TRY THIS Create a new page with the template you created. On the Insert tab, click Page Templates. In the Templates pane, open the My Templates category and click your template's name.

Choose the default page template for section pages

1 On the ribbon, click the Insert tab.

2 In the Pages group, click Page Templates.

3 In the Templates pane, click the Always Use A Specific Template list.

4 Select a default template for this section.

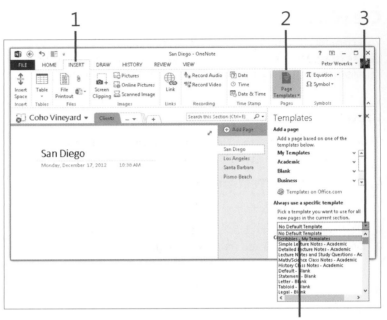

Creating page groups

A page and its subpages is called a *page group*. Create sub-pages in a page group to store information that is subordinate to information on a page. You can see which pages in a page group are the subpages because they are indented on the page tabs. As well as turning pages into subpages, you can turn sub-pages into pages.

Create a page group

1 Right-click the page tab of the page that you want to be the first subpage in the page group.

2 On the shortcut menu that appears, click Make Subpage.

The page's tab is indented to show that it is a subpage.

3 Alternatively, drag the page tab of the page that you want to be a subpage to the right to create a subpage.

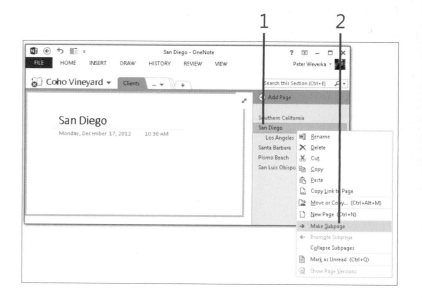

 TRY THIS Right-click a subpage and then, on the shortcut menu that appears, choose Promote Subpage (or drag the subpage tab to the left) to turn the subpage into a page.

TIP You can create sub-subpages. You can indent pages as far as necessary to organize them in different ways.

Expanding or collapsing pages in a group

You can collapse the subpages in a OneNote 2013 page group to hide the page tabs temporarily. After collapsing the subpages, you can easily move or copy all the pages in the group with the Move or Copy command or by dragging. You can expand the subpages to redisplay their page tabs again.

On the page tabs, the names of subpages are indented. When you move the pointer over the first page tab in a page group, the Expand/Collapse button appears on its page tab. You can click this button to expand or collapse subpages.

Expand and collapse pages in a group

1 Click the Collapse button (the upward-pointing arrow) on the first page of a page group to hide the subpages.

2 Click the page group's Expand button (the downward-pointing arrow) to display the subpages.

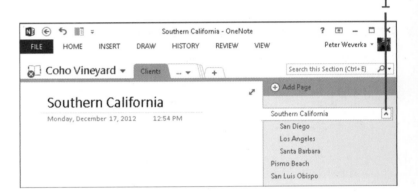

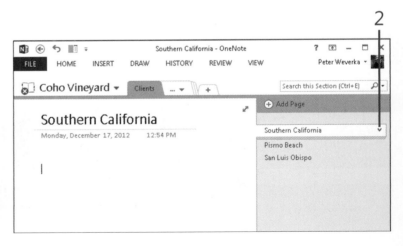

TIP You can also use these techniques to collapse or expand subpages:

- Right-click any page tab in the group and then, on the shortcut menu that appears, click Collapse Subpages or Expand Subpages.

- Press Ctrl+Shift+*.

Revisiting and restoring a different version of a page

OneNote 2013 keeps back-copies of pages in case you want to revisit or restore an earlier version of a page. After you open a version of a page, you can restore it, making it the primary copy, or copy it to another section.

What's more, you can delete a version of a page, or all the versions of pages in a section, section group, or an entire notebook. You can also instruct OneNote not to keep page versions in a notebook. On the History tab, you can click the Page Versions button to open a pane, in which you'll find commands for deleting versions of a page in a section, section group, or notebook, and for disabling the back-copying of pages.

Revisit and restore a page version

1 Open the page that you want to revisit.

2 On the ribbon, click the History tab.

3 In the History group, click Page Versions.

4 Select the tab of a page version that you want to review.

(continued on next page)

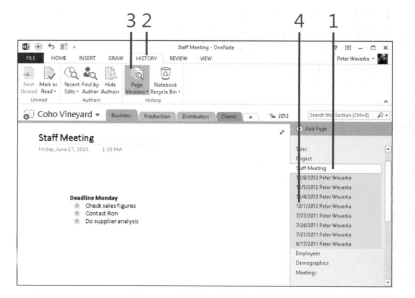

Revisit and restore a page version *(continued)*

5 Examine the earlier version of the page.

6 Click the Information bar to open the page version menu.

7 From the menu that appears, choose Restore Version.

8 On the ribbon, click Page Versions again (this button is a toggle, and clicking it again hides the page versions).

> ✓ **TIP** After you restore an earlier version of a page, the version that was formerly the current version is added to the page versions list so that you can restore it if need be.

> 🔍 **SEE ALSO** To learn how to copy a version of a page to a different section (start by choosing Copy Page To), read "Moving or copying pages" on page 160.

Delete page versions

1 On the ribbon, click the History tab.

2 In the History group, click Page Versions.

3 From the menu that appears, choose Delete All Versions In Section.

> ✓ **TIP** To delete individual versions of a page, click the Page Versions button. Then, in the page tabs, right-click the version that you want to delete and click Delete Version.

> ✓ **TIP** To stop keeping versions of pages throughout a notebook, click Page Versions and choose Disable History For This Notebook. Beware, however, that choosing this command instructs OneNote not to keep backup copies of the notebook itself as well as its pages.

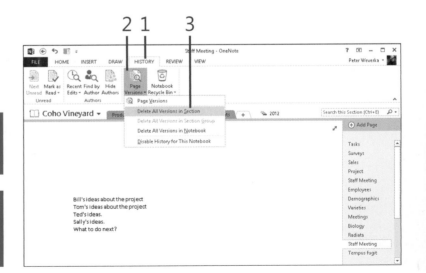

Password-protecting a section

You can password-protect a OneNote 2013 section if you want to control who can read its pages. Before you password-protect a section, consider these password restrictions:

- To search password-protected sections, you must open them first and conduct your search within ten minutes of opening (you can change this setting on the Advanced tab in the OneNote Options dialog box).

- You can't share password-protected sections with OneNote Web App or OneNote mobile apps.

- Passwords are case-sensitive (you must enter, and remember, the right combination of uppercase and lowercase letters).

Password-protect a section

1 Right-click the section tab of the section to which you want apply a password.

2 On the shortcut menu that appears, click Password Protect This Section.

3 In the Password Protection pane, click Set Password.

(continued on next page)

Password-protect a section *(continued)*

4   In the Password Protection dialog box, in the Enter Password text box, type a password. Type it again in the Confirm Password text box for confirmation purposes and click OK.

5   If the Existing Section Backups dialog box appears, click Delete Existing Backups. (Because previous backups were not password protected, you'll want to remove them.)

> ✔ **TIP** To determine how long sections are unlocked and available for editing after you enter the password, click the File tab and choose Options. Then, in the Advanced category of the OneNote Options dialog box, choose a setting from the Lock Password Protected Sections After I Have Worked On Them menu.

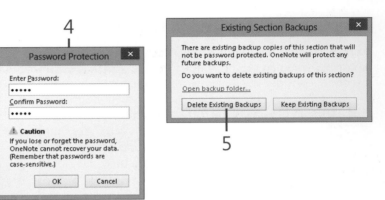

Open a password-protected section

1   Click the tab of the password-protected section that you want to open.

2   Click on the page or press Enter.

3   In the Protected Section dialog box, enter the password.

4   Click OK.

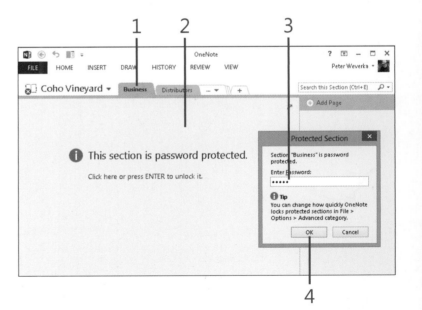

Removing a password from a section

If you no longer need to protect a section in OneNote 2013 with a password, you can remove it. Removing a password makes the section available for viewing by anyone who has access to it. You must know the password to remove it from a section.

Remove a password from a section

1 Right-click the tab of the section whose password you want to remove.

2 On the shortcut menu that appears, click Password Protect This Section.

3 In the Password Protection pane, click Remove Password.

4 In the Remove Password dialog box, type the password and click OK.

TIP To change a password, in the Password Protection pane, click the Change Password button, enter the old password, enter the new password twice, and then click OK.

Writing basic notes

4

The simplest type of note is a typewritten note—one you enter with the keyboard. Entering this kind of note is simple because all you need to do is click on a page and start typing.

Pages tend to become crowded with notes, and to prevent that from happening, you can move notes and delete the ones you no longer need.

The standard techniques for copying and moving text in Microsoft Office 2013 also apply in Microsoft OneNote 2013. For example, on the ribbon, on the Home tab, you'll find the Cut, Copy, and Paste buttons. You'll find standard commands for formatting text there as well, including the Font menu, Bold button, and Italic button. And, like Microsoft Word 2013 and Microsoft PowerPoint 2013, OneNote has a Style menu for quickly formatting text.

Do you want to to create a numbered or bulleted list? You can do that in OneNote 2013, too, by using the Bullets and Numbering buttons on the Home tab.

In this section:

- Writing a note with the keyboard
- Changing alignment and spacing in a note
- Moving notes
- Deleting notes
- Entering symbols and unusual letters
- Selecting text
- Copying and moving text
- Formatting text
- Applying styles to text
- Creating numbered and bulleted lists

Writing a note with the keyboard

To write a note in OneNote 2013, all you need to do is click on a page and start typing. OneNote creates a note container for each note that you write. As you write, the note container changes size to accommodate the text. A note can be as short or long as you want it to be.

Write a note

1 Click on a page and type some text.

2 Press the Enter key to start a new paragraph.

3 Continue typing and notice how the note container widens to accommodate the text. When the container is as wide as it can be, the text wraps to next line.

4 Make the note container wider or narrower by moving the pointer over the sizing handle (located on the upper-right corner of the note container); when the pointer changes to a double-headed arrow, drag to the right to make the note wider or the left to make it narrower.

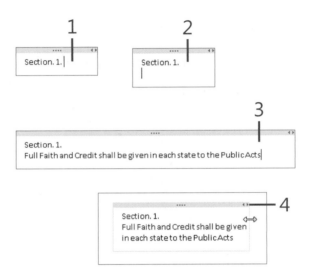

> **TRY THIS** Type a paragraph or two to create a note. Resize the note container and watch what happens when you make the container narrower and then wider again.

Changing alignment and spacing in a note

A note is similar to a page in a Word 2013 document in that you can add paragraphs and align them in different ways. You can also control how much space appears between paragraphs.

The following tables describe paragraph-alignment and paragraph-spacing options.

Paragraph alignment options	
Align Left	Aligns the paragraph along the left side of the note container
Center	Centers the paragraph within the note container
Align Right	Aligns the paragraph along the right side of the note container

Paragraph spacing options	
Align Left	Aligns the paragraph along the left side of the note container
Center	Centers the paragraph within the note container
Align Right	Aligns the paragraph along the right side of the note container
Before	Determines the amount of blank space above the paragraph (enter the amount of space in points)
After	Determines the amount of blank space below the paragraph (in points)
Line Spacing At Least	Determines the amount of space (in points) of lines in a multiline paragraph, taking into account the font size. The height of lines is automatically adjusted to fit the largest-sized character, but you can use this setting to increase the line height. Use this setting to double or triple-space paragraphs. For example, in a paragraph whose text size is 11 points, enter 22 to double-space the text; enter 33 to triple-space the text. This spacing also affects the first line of a paragraph, effectively adding space above the paragraph.

Change alignment and spacing in a note

1 Click anywhere in the paragraph that you want to change.

2 On the ribbon, click the Home tab.

3 In the Paragraph group, click Paragraph Alignment.

4 In the drop-down menu that appears, click a paragraph alignment.

You can choose Align Left, Center, or Align Right.

5 Click Paragraph Alignment again to change spacing before, after, or within a paragraph.

6 Click Paragraph Spacing Options.

The Paragraph Spacing dialog box opens.

7 Enter the spacing you want in the Before, After, and/or Line Spacing At Least box and click OK.

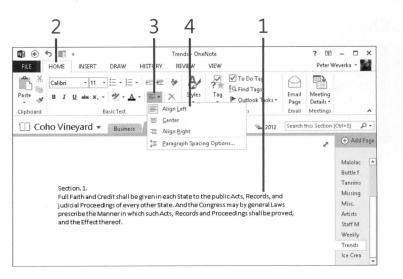

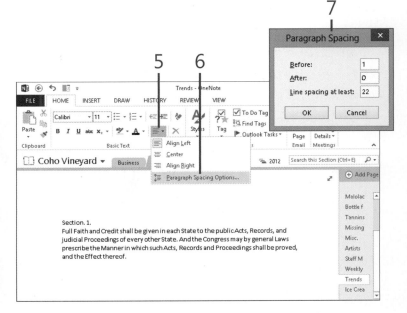

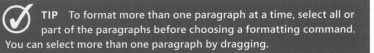

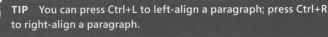

TIP To format more than one paragraph at a time, select all or part of the paragraphs before choosing a formatting command. You can select more than one paragraph by dragging.

TIP You can press Ctrl+L to left-align a paragraph; press Ctrl+R to right-align a paragraph.

SEE ALSO To learn how to write notes with a pen device, read "Handwriting notes and converting them to text" on page 79.

Moving notes

As a page starts to get crowded with notes, you might need to move the notes around to more clearly read them or to resize them. Rather than drag notes one at a time to move them, you can select several at once and move them. You can also click the Insert Space button and drag to increase or decrease the space between notes.

Before you can move a note, you must select it. The trick to selecting a note is to move the mouse pointer over the bar along its top and then click. You can see when the pointer is over this bar because it turns into the four-headed arrow pointer.

Move notes

1   Move the pointer over the bar along the top of a note; to select the note, click when you see the four-headed pointer. To move a note by touch, tap the move handle (located at the top center of the note container).

2   Ctrl+click the note bars or Ctrl+tap the move handles on more than one note to select them.

3   Drag the notes to a different location.

4   On the ribbon, click the Insert tab.

5   Click Insert Space to visually adjust the space between notes.

6   Drag downward on the page to insert space and move the notes further down. Drag upward to move the notes closer together.

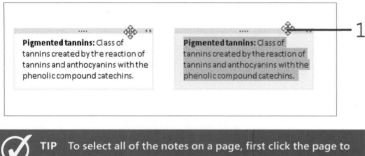

> **TIP**   To select all of the notes on a page, first click the page to make sure that no notes are selected and then press Ctrl+A.

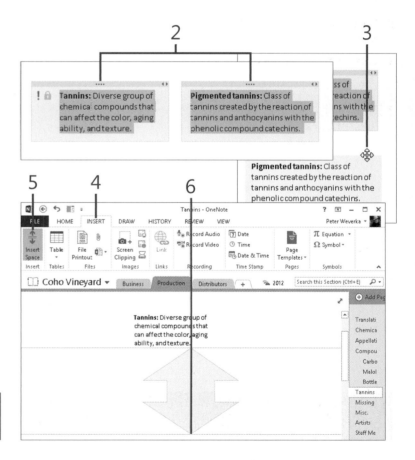

Deleting notes

You can delete unwanted notes to make a page less crowded or to get rid of notes that you no longer need.

You can delete one or more notes a time. Before you can delete a note, you have to select it. The trick to selecting a note is to click the bar along its top. You can tell when the pointer is over this bar because it turns into the four-headed arrow pointer.

Delete a note

1 Move the pointer over the bar along the top of a note; to select the note, click when you see the four-headed pointer. To move a note by touch, tap the move handle (located at the top center of the note container).

2 On the ribbon, click the Home tab.

3 In the Basic Text group, click Delete.

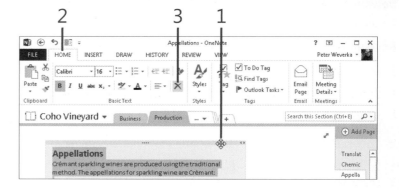

Delete multiple notes

1 Ctrl+click the note bars or Ctrl+tap the move handles on more than one note to select them.

2 Right-click the bar along the top of a note and click Delete (or press the Delete key) to delete the notes you selected.

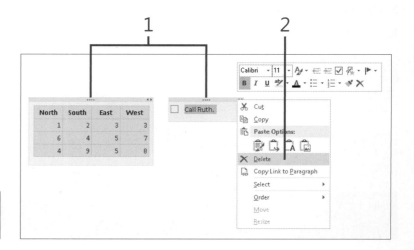

> ✓ **TIP** To select all the notes on a page, click the page to make sure that no notes are selected and then press Ctrl+A.

Entering symbols and unusual characters

What do you do when you need to enter a symbol or unusual character into a note that isn't on the keyboard? For those times, look to the Symbol gallery and Symbol dialog box.

The Symbol gallery lists the previous 20 characters and symbols you entered. If the character or symbol you need isn't there, you can probably find it the Symbol dialog box.

Enter a symbol or unusual character

1 On the ribbon, click the Insert tab.

2 In the Symbols group, click Symbol.

The Symbol gallery opens.

3 Click a symbol or character in the gallery to insert it in a note.

4 If the symbol you need is not in the gallery, click More Symbols.

The Symbol dialog box opens.

5 Scroll through the Symbol dialog box and select a symbol or character.

6 Click Insert.

7 Click Close to dismiss the Symbol dialog box.

> **TRY THIS** Click Symbol and notice that the symbol or character you just chose is now on the gallery in case you want to choose it again.

> **TRY THIS** If you know a character's Unicode character code, you can enter the character without opening the Symbol dialog box by entering the code and then pressing Alt+X. For example, enter type 00BD and press Alt+X to enter the character ½. To find a Unicode character code, select a symbol or character in the Symbol dialog box and note its character code (it's listed near the bottom of the dialog box).

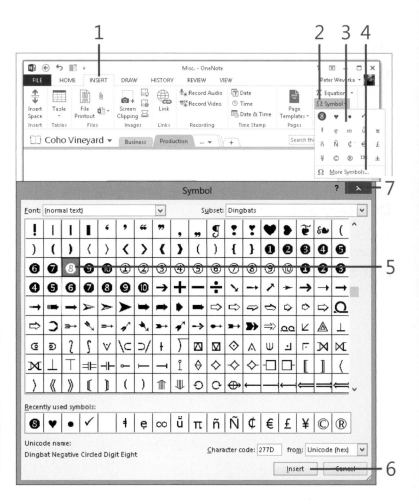

Selecting text

Before you can do anything to text in a note—copy it, move it, or reformat it—you must select it. OneNote offers a handful of techniques for selecting text with the mouse. To select text by touch, tap the text and drag the selection handle.

To select	Do this
A word	Double-click the word
Some text	Drag across the text
To the beginning of a line	Press Shift+Home
To the end of a line	Press Shift+End
Current paragraph and subordinate paragraphs (if any)	Click the paragraph handle or press Ctrl+Shift+- (Control+Shift+hyphen) to select a paragraph and any subordinate paragraphs (created as part of an outline). Click the paragraph handle or press Ctrl+Shift+- again to select only the current paragraph.

You can tell when text is selected because OneNote highlights it.

Select text

1 Double-click a word in a note to select it. To select a word by touch, tap the word and drag the selection handle.

2 Drag across some text to select more than one word, or tap the text and drag the selection handle.

(continued on next page)

1

Section. 3.
New States may be admitted by the Congress into this Union; but no new State shall be formed or erected within the Jurisdiction of any other State; nor any State be formed by the Junction of two or more States, or Parts of States, without the Consent of the Legislatures of the States concerned as well Congress.

2

Section. 3.
New States may be admitted by the Congress into this Union; but no new State shall be formed or erected within the Jurisdiction of any other State; nor any State be formed by the Junction of two or more States, or Parts of States, without the Consent of the Legislatures of the States concerned as well as of the Congress.

Select text *(continued)*

3 Press Ctrl+Shift+- (Control+Shift+hyphen) to select the current paragraph (you might need to click in a paragraph first) and any subordinate paragraphs.

4 Click a paragraph handle to select the paragraph and any subordinate paragraphs (the paragraph handle appears when you move the pointer over a paragraph). Click the paragraph handle again to select only the current paragraph.

3

Section.3.

New States may be admitted by the Congress into this Union; but no new State shall be formed or erected within the Jurisdiction of any other State; nor any State be formed by the Junction of two or more States, or Parts of States, without the Consent of the Legislatures of the States concerned as well as of the Congress.

4 —

Section.3.

New States may be admitted by the Congress into this Union; but no new State shall be formed or erected within the Jurisdiction of any other State; nor any State be formed by the Junction of two or more States, or Parts of States, without the Consent of the Legislatures of the States concerned as well as of the Congress.

 SEE ALSO To learn how to use the paragraph handle to manipulate an item in an outline, read "Creating and constructing outlines" on page 81.

TIP You can also triple-click a paragraph to select it and any subordinate paragraphs.

TIP After you select a note container, you can copy, move, delete, or format its text. To select a note container, click the bar along its top or tap its move handle.

Copying and moving text

OneNote offers a number of ways to copy and move text from one place to another in a note and from one note to another. After you select the text, you can use the buttons on the Home tab or the commands on the shortcut menu to copy or move it. You can also drag the text to move it.

Copying and moving text with the Copy and Cut buttons (or their keyboard shortcuts) entails copying text to the Windows clipboard and then pasting it by using a Paste command.

Button	Shortcut key	Description
Copy	Ctrl+C	Copy selected text to the clipboard.
Cut	Ctrl+X	Cut selected text to the clipboard.
Paste	Ctrl+V	Paste text from the clipboard. OneNote offers these options for pasting: **Keep Source Formatting** The text keeps its original formatting. **Merge Formatting** The text blends with the formatting of the text into which it is copied or moved. **Keep Text Only** The text is stripped of all formatting. **Picture** The text is rendered in the form of a graphic.

Copy text

1 On the ribbon, click the Home tab.

2 Select text in a note.

3 In the Clipboard group, click the Copy icon (or press Ctrl+C) to copy the text to the clipboard.

4 Click a different location in the note.

5 Right-click, and then on the shortcut menu that appears, choose a Paste command.

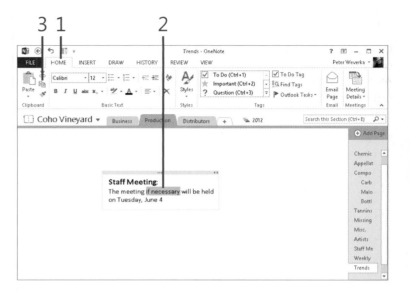

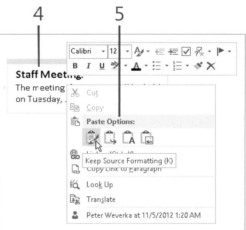

 SEE ALSO To learn how to select text in a note, see "Selecting text" on page 62.

TIP Don't forget the shortcut keys for cutting (Ctrl+X), copying (Ctrl+C), and pasting text (Ctrl+V). These shortcut keys can come in very handy.

Move text

1   On the ribbon, click the Home tab.

2   Select text in a note.

3   In the Clipboard group, click the Cut icon (or press Ctrl+C).

4   Click a different location.

5   Click Paste to paste the text with its original formatting or click the arrow on the Paste button to choose a different option.

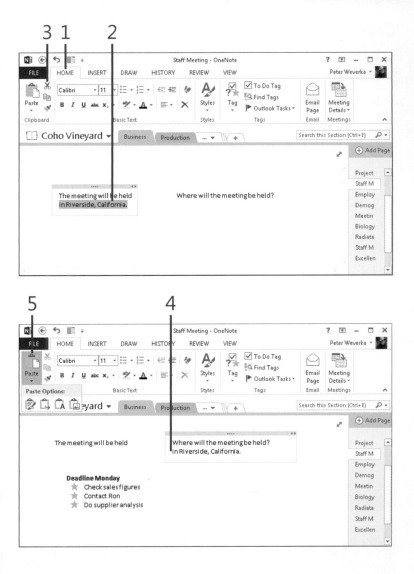

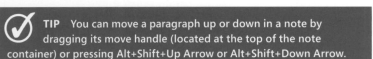

TIP   You can move a paragraph up or down in a note by dragging its move handle (located at the top of the note container) or pressing Alt+Shift+Up Arrow or Alt+Shift+Down Arrow.

SEE ALSO   To learn how to select text in a note, see "Selecting text" on page 62.

Formatting text

Take a look at the Basic Text group on the Home tab to see the different tools for formatting text in notes. Do these tools look familiar? If you have any experience with Microsoft Word, you probably recognize the Font menu, Font Size menu, and Font Style buttons (Bold, Italic, Underline, and Strikethrough). The formatting tools and their shortcut keys work the same way in OneNote and Word.

OneNote gives you these methods to format text:

Menu/button	Shortcut key	Description
Font		Choose a font (a typeface)
Font Size		Shrink or enlarge the text
Bold	Ctrl+B	**Boldface** the text
Italic	Ctrl+I	*Italicize* the text
Underline	Ctrl+U	<u>Underline</u> the text
Strikethrough	Ctrl+-	Draw a line through the text
Subscript/Superscript	Ctrl+=; Ctrl+Shift+=	Reduce the font size and lower or raise the text from the baseline (the imaginary line on which the letters rest)
Text Highlight Color	Ctrl+Alt+H	Highlight text with the currently selected highlighter
Font Color		Change the color of text

To use the formatting tools, do one of the following:

- Select a formatting option and then start typing.
- Select the text first and then select a formatting option.

OneNote offers a special button for stripping all formats from text: the Clear All Formatting button, which is located in the upper-right corner of the Basic Text group (or press Ctrl+Shift+N). Use this button to wipe the slate clean, so to speak, and start all over with formatting text.

Format text

1 On the ribbon, click the Home tab.

2 Select the text that you want to format.

3 Click Bold, Italic, Underline, Strikethrough, or Subscript/Superscript to apply any of those text effects.

4 Open the Font menu and choose a different font.

(continued on next page)

1 3   2

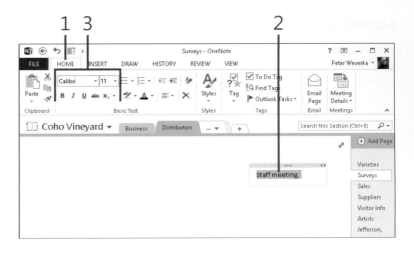

4

Format text *(continued)*

5 Open the Font Size menu and choose a different size for the text.

6 Open the Font Color menu and choose a different color for the text.

(continued on next page)

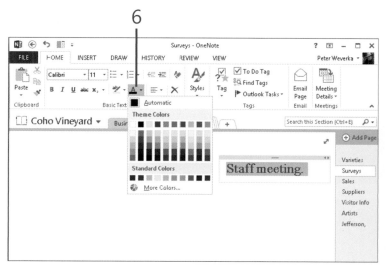

Format text *(continued)*

7 Click Text Highlight Color and choose a highlight color to highlight the text. To remove the color from highlighted text, choose No Color.

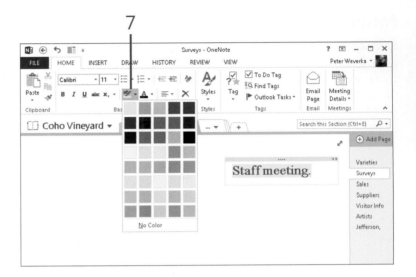

TIP To remove formatting from selected text, on the Home tab, in the Basic Text group, click the Clear All Formatting button (or press Ctrl+Shift+N).

TIP A quick way to format text is to use the Format Painter. Click in text that is formatted using the styles that you want to apply elsewhere. Then, on the Home tab, in the Clipboard group, click the Format Painter button once and click a word or drag across the text to which you want to copy the formats. To quit the Format Painter, click its button or press Esc.

SEE ALSO To learn how to format text quickly with a style, see "Applying styles to text" on page 71.

Applying styles to text

The fastest way to reformat text in a note is to apply a style. OneNote offers 11 styles in all. Six of the styles (Heading 1 through Heading 6) are for formatting headings. Normal is the default style, the one that is used when you create a new note. OneNote also provides the Page Title style for page titles, the Citation style for citations, the Quote style for quotations, and the Code style for computer code. However, you can use these styles any way you want.

Styles apply to entire paragraphs, not to individual words or letters. To apply a style, just click in a paragraph and choose a style.

OneNote offers these keyboard shortcuts for applying styles:

Press	To apply this style
Ctrl+Alt+1 through Ctrl+Alt+6	Heading 1 through 6
Ctrl+Shift+N	Normal

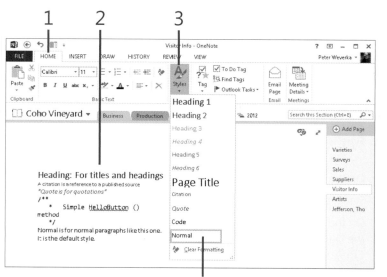

Apply styles to text

1 On the ribbon, click the Home tab.

2 Click in a paragraph.

3 On the ribbon, click Styles.

4 Choose a style.

 TIP To apply a style to more than one paragraph, select the paragraphs before applying the style.

⚠ **CAUTION** Styles override other text formats. When you apply a style, formats in the style take precedence over formats that are already there (such as bold or italics), and the formats that were already there are lost.

Creating numbered and bulleted lists

Lists are invaluable for keeping information in notes. You can use numbered lists to rank items in a list or describe step-by-step instructions. Use bulleted lists to present alternatives or to list unranked items.

In OneNote, you don't have to enter the numbers or bullets yourself. After you click the Numbering or Bullets button on the Home tab, OneNote numbers the list or applies bullets for you. You can choose from several numbering schemes and bullet styles.

To create a numbered or bulleted list, use one of these techniques:

- Enter items for the list. (Note that each item must be in its own paragraph.) Select the items and then apply the bulleted or numbered list format.

- Select a bulleted or numbered list format and then enter list items. Each time you press the Enter key to start a new line, OneNote applies a number or bullet to the list item. Press Enter twice to end the list.

On the shortcut menu, OneNote offers commands for starting new lists, continuing previous lists, removing numbers or bullets from an item in the list, and changing numbered lists to bulleted lists, and vice versa.

Create a numbered list

1 Type several items for a list, pressing Enter after you enter each item. Do not type the numbers; OneNote numbers the items for you.

2 On the ribbon, click the Home tab.

3 Select the list items.

4 On the ribbon, in the Basic Text group, click the down-arrow on the Numbering button. (If you click the Numbering button or press Ctrl+/, the default numbering style is applied.)

The Numbering gallery opens.

5 Choose a numbering scheme.

TIP Open the gallery on the Numbering button and choose None (or press Ctrl+/) to remove all numbers from the list.

Create a bulleted list

1 Type several items for a list, pressing Enter after you enter each item.

2 On the ribbon, click the Home tab.

3 Select the items in the list.

4 On the ribbon, in the Basic Text group, click the down-arrow on the Bullets button. (If you click the Bullets button or press Ctrl+, the default bullet style is applied.)

5 Choose a bullet style.

TRY THIS Type 1. and press the Spacebar. OneNote automatically creates a numbered list for you. After you enter the first list item and press Enter, OneNote enters a "2" for the second item in the list. You can use this automatic technique to create numbered lists. Press Enter twice to end the list.

SEE ALSO To learn how to create another kind of numbered list, an outline, see "Creating and constructing outlines" on page 81.

TRY THIS Type an asterisk (*) and press the Spacebar. OneNote automatically creates a bulleted list. After you enter list items and press Enter, OneNote attaches a bullet to each item on the list. You can use this simple method to create bulleted lists.

Taking notes to another level

Typewritten notes aren't the only kind of notes that you can write. Far from it. You can also handwrite notes and convert them to text, record audio notes, and record video notes.

Microsoft OneNote 2013 also comes with special tools for constructing outlines and math equations.

To include information from other sources, consider attaching a file to a note, copying contents to a note as a file printout, and scanning documents and placing the scanned images in notes.

OneNote 2013 makes it easy to insert pictures and screenshots in notes, too.

When you're in a hurry to write a note or you haven't decided yet where to store one, write a quick note. You can store quick notes temporarily in the Quick Notes section until you find a permanent place for them.

In this section:

- Writing quick notes
- Reading, moving, and deleting quick notes
- Handwriting notes and converting them to text
- Creating and constructing outlines
- Attaching a file or copying a file's contents to a note
- Inserting a picture from your computer or network
- Inserting a picture from an Internet source
- Taking a screen clipping
- Constructing simple math equations
- Recording audio and video notes
- Playing back audio and video notes

Writing quick notes

When you want to jot down a note but can't decide where to store it, or you want to jot down a note without first opening OneNote 2013, write a *quick note*. (In versions of OneNote prior to 2013, quick notes were called side notes.) After you write a quick note, it is stored in the Quick Notes section (located below the list of open notebooks in the Notebooks pane) until you delete it or move it to a page or section in a notebook.

Write quick notes in the Quick Note window. This window offers the Home, Insert, Draw, View, and Pages tabs for formatting and handling the quick notes you write. Click the Close button to close the Quick Note window after you write your quick note.

Write a quick note

1 In the notification area on the right side of the Windows taskbar, click the Send To OneNote icon. (If you don't see the Send To One-Note icon, in the notification area, click Show Hidden Icons.)

2 In the Send To OneNote window, click New Quick Note.

3 Write a quick note.

4 Continue to add to the note as needed. Click Close when you finish writing the note.

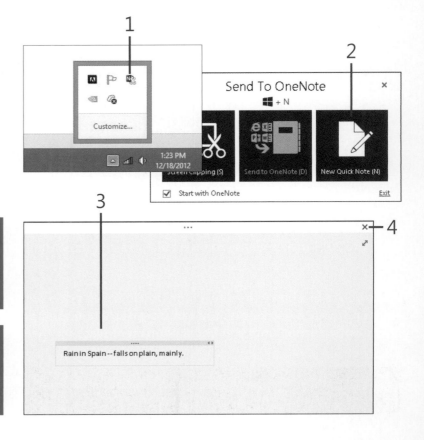

> ✓ **TIP** You can also open the Send To OneNote window by clicking the Send To OneNote button on the View tab in OneNote or pressing Windows key+N. Also, if OneNote is open, the Send To OneNote icon might appear on the taskbar. Click it to open the Send To OneNote window.

> ✓ **TIP** If the Send to OneNote icon doesn't appear in the notification area, click File and then, in the Backstage view, click the Options tab. In the OneNote Options dialog box, click Display, select the Place OneNote Icon In The Notification Area Of The Taskbar check box, and then click OK.

Format a quick note

1 In the Quick Note window, click the Auto-Hide Ribbon button (the ellipsis character at the top of the window) to display the ribbon.

2 Select some text in the quick note.

3 Format the text by using a command on the Home tab.

4 Click Close.

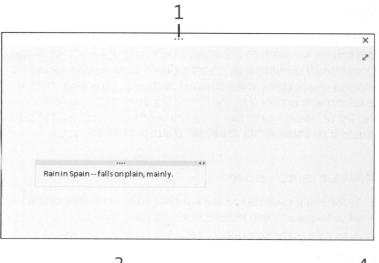

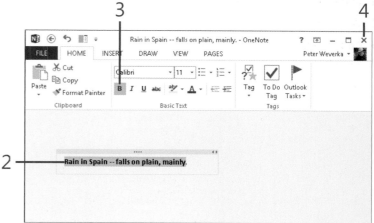

SEE ALSO To learn how to move a quick note to a notebook, see "Reading, moving, and deleting quick notes" on page 78.

Reading, moving, and deleting quick notes

Quick notes are kept in the Quick Notes section until you delete them or move them to a different section or page. To open the Quick Notes section, open OneNote 2013 (if necessary) and then, at the bottom of the Notebooks pane, click Quick Notes.

Quick notes are stored one to a page in the Quick Notes section. Click a page in the page tabs to read a quick note. The name of each quick note appears on a page tab. OneNote gets these names from the first bit of text in a quick note.

Read, move, and delete quick notes

1 At the bottom of the Notebooks pane, click Quick Notes.

2 To read a quick note, click a page tab.

3 To move a quick note to a section in an open notebook, drag a page tab to a section in the Notebooks pane.

4 To delete a quick note, right-click a page tab and then, on the shortcut menu that appears, click Delete.

TRY THIS Edit a quick note. You can edit quick notes just like other notes. Click the quick note's page tab to display its contents and make your changes. You can insert a picture, draw in the note, or do any note-related task. Changes are saved automatically.

Handwriting notes and converting them to text

If you have a tablet, touch-enabled computer, or pen device, you can handwrite notes. In fact, if handwriting notes is easier for you, or if you share your notebooks with a collaborator and you believe handwritten notes are less formal, you might prefer to handwrite all your notes. To handwrite a note, select a pen, and drag your finger or pen device on the pad or screen. (You can also, with unsatisfactory results, handwrite notes by dragging the mouse.)

You can convert handwritten notes to text. OneNote identifies each character as you write, then converts the result to typed text. You can edit this converted text just like typed text.

Handwrite a note

1   On the ribbon, click the Draw tab.

2   In the Tools group, in the Pens gallery, select a pen.

3   Using your finger, a pen device, or the mouse, drag to handwrite a note.

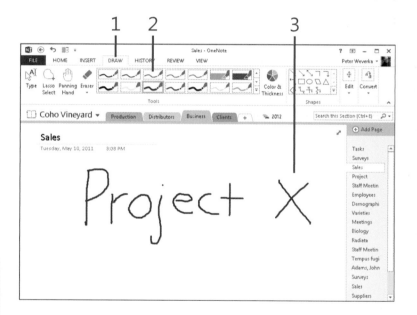

> **SEE ALSO**   To learn how to choose a pen size and pen color for drawing and handwriting notes, read "Drawing free-form with a pen or highlighter" on page 146.

> ⚠ **CAUTION**   If you can't handwrite notes, OneNote isn't in Create Handwriting Only mode or Create Both Handwriting and Drawings mode. To change pen modes, open the Pens gallery, click Pen Mode, and then choose either Create Handwriting Only mode or Create Both Handwriting and Drawings.

Convert a handwritten note to text

1 Select the handwritten note that you want to convert to text.

2 In the Convert group, click Ink To Text.

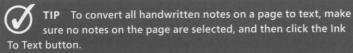

⚠ **CAUTION** You can't import handwritten text into OneNote and then convert it to text.

Creating and constructing outlines

An outline is a list of important topics on a given subject. In a typical outline, topics are listed at different levels, with first-level topics not indented and sublevel topics indented to show they are subordinate.

To help construct outlines, OneNote 2013 offers the paragraph handle. Move the pointer over a topic in the outline list to display its paragraph handle, which appears on the left, and then do the following to construct an outline:

- **Change the outline level (the amount of indentation)** Drag the paragraph handle to the left or right to change the topic's outline level. Dragging the handle to the right lowers the outline level; dragging the handle to the left raises it. You can also press Tab or, on the Home tab, click the Increase Indent Position button to move a topic to a lower level; press Shift+Tab or click the Decrease Indent Position button to raise a subtopic to a higher level.

- **Move a topic up or down in the outline** Drag the paragraph handle up or down in the note.

- **Select a topic and its subtopics** Click the paragraph handle.

- **Collapse or expand a topic's subtopics** Double-click the paragraph handle. You can also press Alt+Shift+minus sign to collapse or Alt+Shift+plus sign to expand subtopics.

- **Select topics at different levels** Right-click the paragraph handle and then, on the shortcut menu that appears, point to Select. On the submenu that appears, choose a level. Select all topics on the same level when you want to format text. For example, to italicize all level-3 subtopics, select them and click the Italic button.

Create and construct an outline

1 Create the initial outline as a list.

2 Select the items in the outline and press Ctrl+/ (or, on the Home tab, click the Numbering button) to number the outline. You can open the gallery on the Numbering button and select an alternative numbering scheme, such as a., b., c., or I., II., III.

(continued on next page)

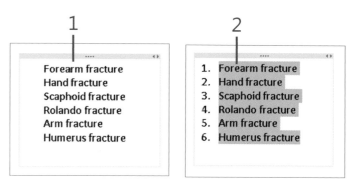

Create and construct an outline (continued)

3 Drag to select the items in the outline that you want to make subordinate.

4 Drag the paragraph handle next to one of the items to the right to indent the selected items.

5 Double-click an item's paragraph handle to collapse its subtopics.

6 Drag an item's paragraph handle upward to move that item higher in the outline.

7 Double-click the paragraph handle on a collapsed item to expand it.

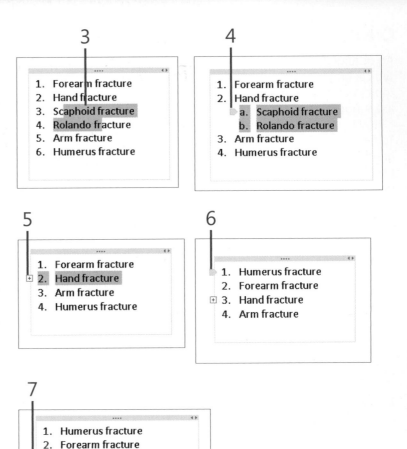

3

1. Forearm fracture
2. Hand fracture
3. Scaphoid fracture
4. Rolando fracture
5. Arm fracture
6. Humerus fracture

4

1. Forearm fracture
2. Hand fracture
   a. Scaphoid fracture
   b. Rolando fracture
3. Arm fracture
4. Humerus fracture

5

1. Forearm fracture
2. Hand fracture
3. Arm fracture
4. Humerus fracture

6

1. Humerus fracture
2. Forearm fracture
3. Hand fracture
4. Arm fracture

7

1. Humerus fracture
2. Forearm fracture
3. Hand fracture
   a. Scaphoid fracture
   b. Rolando fracture
4. Arm fracture

TRY THIS Drag the paragraph handle upward and to the right to indent *and* move a topic in an outline at the same time.

Date-stamping and time-stamping notes

You can date-stamp and time-stamp notes to record when they were written so that have a record of when you took the notes. Or, use the date- and time-stamping commands to insert the current date, time, or date and time in the middle of a note you're writing.

Date-stamp and time-stamp a note

1 On the ribbon, click the Insert tab.

2 To insert the current date, in the Time Stamp group, click Date or press Alt+Shift+D.

3 To insert the current time, click Time or press Alt+Shift+T.

4 To insert the current date and time, click Date & Time or press Alt+Shift+F.

TIP To insert your name along with the current date and current time in a note, right-click the note and then, on the shortcut menu that appears, click the last option (for example, choose Joe Jones at 1/12/13 3:02 PM).

TRY THIS You can always tell when a note was written (and who wrote it). Right-click the paragraph handle on a note. On the shortcut menu that appears, the last entry lists the author's name along with the date and the time that the note was written.

Attaching a file or copying a file's content to a note

Attach a file to a note to preserve a copy of a file or make it available in a notebook. After you attach a file to a note, you can double-click its icon to open it. You can also share a file attached to a note by sending the note via email (the attached file is sent along with the note).

You can attach more than one file in a note by using the File Attachment command.

Insert a file printout to copy the text from a file into OneNote and retain all the text formatting. After you insert the text, you can read and search it, but not edit it. Besides inserting the file text, OneNote inserts a shortcut icon to the file and a link to the file. You can double-click the shortcut icon or click the file link to open the file in its default application and edit it as needed.

Attach a file to a note

1   On the ribbon, click the Insert tab.

2   In the Files group, click File Attachment.

3   In the Choose A File Or A Set Of Files To Insert dialog box, select the file to attach. (Ctrl+click to select more than one file).

4   Click Insert.

5   In the Insert File dialog box, choose Attach File.

An icon, linked to a copy of the file, is inserted into the note. Double-click this icon to open the file later.

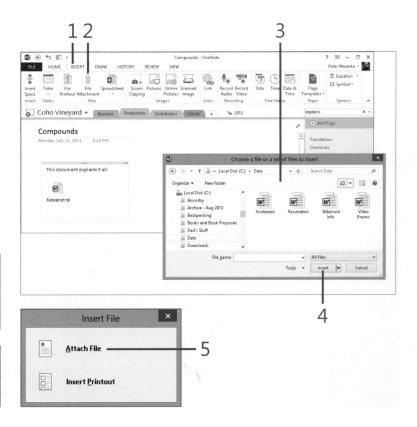

> ⚠ **CAUTION**   Attached files are embedded in notebooks; they are not linked to their original versions. Editorial changes you make to the original file don't appear in the attachment file; likewise, changes you make to the attachment file don't transfer to the original.

> 🔍 **SEE ALSO**   To learn how to link a note to a file so that you can open and edit a file by clicking its link in OneNote, read "Creating a link to a file" on page 120.

Insert a file printout

1 On the ribbon, click the Insert tab.

2 In the Files group, click File Printout.

3 In the Choose Document To Insert dialog box, select the file to copy. You can select multiple files if you want.

4 Click Insert.

The file's text is copied to OneNote, and a link to the file is created.

 TRY THIS Move the pointer over the attached file icon. A ScreenTip shows you the file's name, when it was last modified, the folder from which it was originally copied, and its size.

 TRY THIS Double-click the file printout's shortcut icon to open the file in its default application.

 TRY THIS Make changes to the file you selected in step 3. Save those changes and then return to OneNote. Right-click the file printout icon and then, on the shortcut menu that appears, click Refresh Printout to update OneNote with the changes.

Sending files to OneNote

When you installed Microsoft Office 2013, you installed a virtual printer called Send To OneNote 2013. You can use this virtual printer to copy the text of any file into OneNote, starting in any application. OneNote calls the copied text a "file printout."

The Send To OneNote command doesn't provide a shortcut icon and link to the file along with its copied text in the manner that the File Printout command does, but you can choose which pages of the file to bring into OneNote (the File Printout command does not give you the ability to select the pages you want to copy and place in OneNote).

Send a file to OneNote

1 In the application from which you want to create a file printout, choose the Print command (or press Ctrl+P)

2 In the Print window or Print dialog box, choose the Send To OneNote 2013 printer.

3 Specify a print range (the pages you want to copy to OneNote).

4 Click Print.

   The Select Location In OneNote dialog box appears.

5 In the Select Location In OneNote dialog box, select the page where you want the file printout to go and click OK. To create a new page for the file, select a section.

> **TIP**   To send a Microsoft Word, Microsoft Excel, or Microsoft PowerPoint file printout to OneNote, you can click Send To OneNote on the Windows taskbar and then, in the Send To OneNote window that appears, click Send To OneNote. Doing so opens the Select Location In OneNote dialog box. From there, you can choose a page for the printout.

> **SEE ALSO**   To learn how to create a link to a file in OneNote and be able to click the link to open the file, read "Attaching a file or copying a file's contents to a note" on page 84.

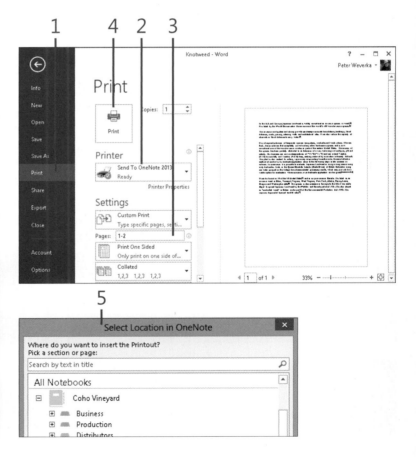

Inserting images from a scanner or digital camera

On the Insert tab, OneNote 2013 offers several commands for placing your own images in notes. Using the Scanned Image command, you can insert content from a scanner or digital camera into a note.

Before using the Scanned Image command, make sure that your scanner or digital camera is plugged into one of your computer's USB ports.

Insert images from a digital camera

1 Click in a note.

2 On the ribbon, click the Insert tab.

3 In the Images group, click Scanned Image.

4 In the Insert Picture From Scanner Or Camera dialog box, in the Device list box, select a device.

5 Click Custom Insert.

6 In the Get Pictures From dialog box, select a photo. To select more than one, Ctrl+click the photos.

7 Click Get Pictures.

The picture(s) you selected are inserted into the note.

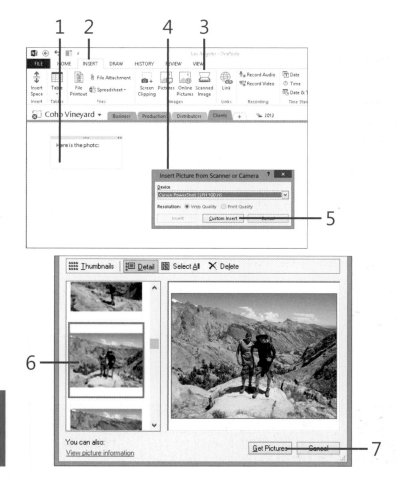

> **TIP** You can change the size of a scanned image. Move the pointer over the lower-right corner. When you see the two-headed arrow, click and start dragging. Drag inward to make the picture smaller; drag outward to make it larger.

Insert images from a scanner

1 Click in a note.

2 On the ribbon, click the Insert tab.

3 In the Images group, click Scanned Image.

4 In the Insert Picture From Scanner Or Camera dialog box, in the Device list box, select a device, and then click the desired resolution option.

5 Click Custom Insert to crop the scanned image and make other adjustments; otherwise, skip this step.

6 Click Insert. (If you clicked Custom Insert in step 4, click Scan instead.)

The scan is inserted into the note where you clicked.

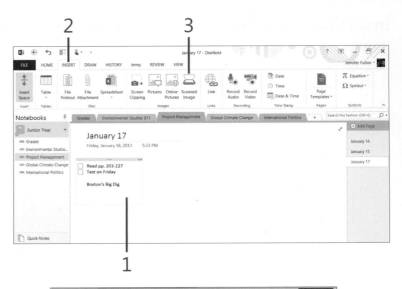

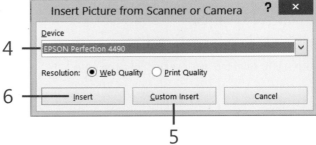

Inserting a picture from your computer or network

Using the Pictures command, you can insert a JPEG, PNG, TIFF, or other digital image from your computer or network into your OneNote 2013 notes.. For that matter, you can insert more than one picture.

Insert a picture from your computer or network

1 Click in a note and then, on the ribbon, click the Insert tab.

2 In the Images group, click Pictures.

3 In the Insert Picture dialog box, select a picture to insert.

4 Click Insert.

The picture you selected is inserted into the note where you clicked.

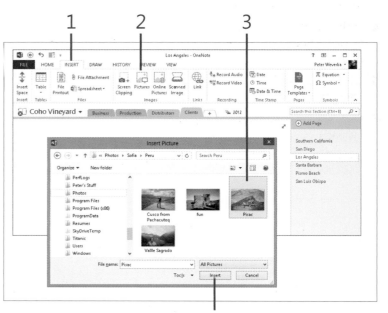

 TIP To select and insert more than one picture, while in the Insert Picture dialog box, Ctrl+click the desired pictures.

SEE ALSO To learn how to insert a picture you keep in a SkyDrive folder, read "Inserting a picture from an Internet source" on page 90.

Inserting a picture from an Internet source

Need a picture to illustrate an idea or concept? You can obtain a picture from an Internet source. OneNote provides the means to search for and obtain pictures from Office.com, the Internet (by way of the Bing search engine), and a SkyDrive folder.

Insert a picture from an Internet source

1 On the ribbon, click the Insert tab.

2 In the Images group, click Online Pictures.

3 In either the Office.com Clip Art or Bing Image Search box, enter a search term that describes the picture that you want and then press Enter. To search your SkyDrive folders, click Browse, instead.

(continued on next page)

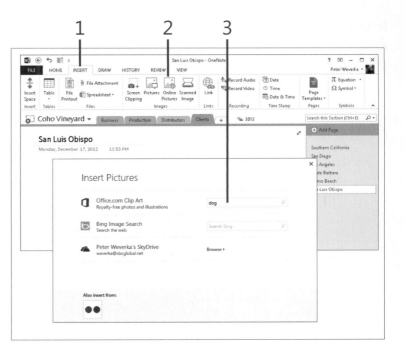

TIP To see a larger view of a picture in the Insert Pictures dialog box, select the picture, move the pointer over it, and then click the View Larger button.

Insert a picture from an Internet
source (continued)

4   Select a picture to insert. (You can select more than one picture if you want.)

5   Click Insert.

4

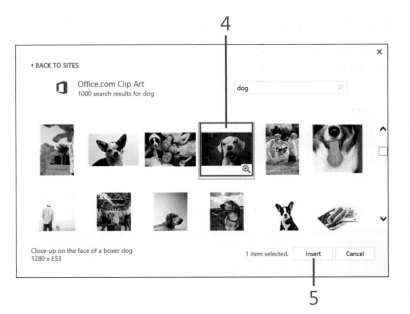

5

 TIP You can also insert a picture from Flickr by clicking the Flickr icon at the bottom of the Insert Pictures dialog box. Follow the onscreen instructions to connect your Microsoft Account to Flickr.

⚠ **CAUTION** You cannot use a picture from a website without first obtaining permission to use it from the website's owner.

✓ **TIP** To change the size of a picture, move the pointer over the lower-right corner. When you see the two-headed arrow, click and start dragging. Drag inward to make the picture smaller; drag outward to enlarge it.

Taking a screen clipping

To capture part of an open window on your computer as a screenshot, take a screen clipping. For example, you can capture part of a webpage or application screen in a screen clipping to preserve it in a OneNote 2013 note or take notes about it.

Before you begin, display the item that you want to capture on your screen. For example, to capture part of a webpage, display the webpage in your browser. Then, switch to OneNote and take the screen clipping.

Take a screen clipping

1 Display the webpage, file, or application window that you want to capture.

(continued on next page)

1

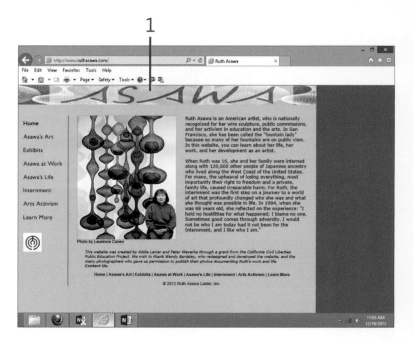

Take a screen clipping (continued)

2 In OneNote, on the ribbon, click the Insert tab.

3 In the Images group, click Screen Clipping.

The screen dims temporarily.

4 Drag on the screen to define the portion of the screen that you want to capture. When you release the mouse button, the area you defined is captured as a screenshot and inserted into the note.

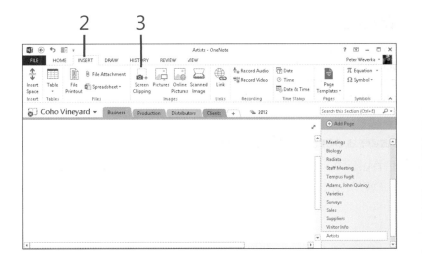

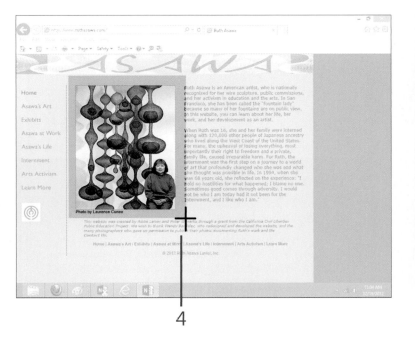

TIP You can also take a screen clipping by using the Send To OneNote tool. On the taskbar, click Send To OneNote. Next, click the Send to OneNote icon in the Windows notification area or press Windows key+S. In the Send To OneNote window, click Screen Clipping. Drag on the screen to define the area that you want to capture. In the Select Location In OneNote dialog box, select the page where you want to place the screen clipping, and then click Send to Selected Location.

TIP If you select the wrong area of the screen, remember that you can click Undo and repeat these steps to try again.

Constructing simple math equations

Writing and drawing math equations can be difficult because of the special symbols that are required. To make constructing equations a little easier, OneNote 2013 offers two techniques for putting equations in notes. To write simple equations, draw the equation in the Insert Ink Equation window. (To see how to build complex equations, read "Constructing complex math equations" on page 95.)

Construct simple equations in the Insert Ink Equation window

1 On the ribbon, click the Draw tab.

2 In the Convert group, click Ink To Math.

3 In the Insert Ink Equation dialog box, using the mouse, a pen device, or your finger, draw an equation.

4 Look at the Preview area to see whether OneNote interpreted your drawing correctly. If not, you can make corrections.

5 Click Insert.

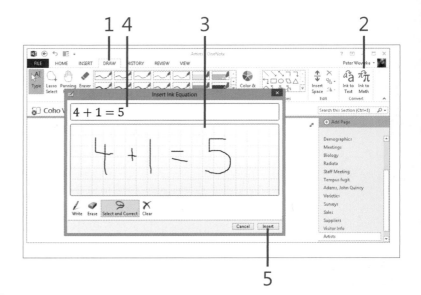

TIP The Insert Ink Equation dialog box offers these tools for constructing equations:

- Click Erase and drag over part of an equation to erase it. Then, click Write to write your correction.

- Click Select And Correct and drag over an equation to repair it. A menu appears with numbers and symbols that you can select to replace what you dragged over.

- Click Clear to remove all edits from the window and start over.

Constructing complex math equations

OneNote 2013 offers two techniques for entering math equations in notes. Writing and drawing complex math equations might seem daunting, but with the special tools OneNote offers, it's relatively easy.

To construct a complex equation, use the Equation Tools Design tab and its special tools. This tab provides mathematical structures and symbols for constructing equations. (To see how to create simple equations, read "Constructing simple math equations" on page 94.)

Construct complex equations by using equation tools

1 On the ribbon, click the Insert tab.

2 In the Symbols group, click Equation.

3 Type your equation.

You don't need to insert spaces between symbols, variables, or numbers. Sometimes it's easier to start with a mathematical structure, and then fill in the blanks. To insert a mathematical structure such as a fraction, script, radical or integral, on the Equation Tools | Design contextual tab, in the Structures group, click the appropriate button. For example, click Fraction and choose a fraction structure in the gallery that appears.

4 Enter the appropriate values in the placeholders. For example, in the fraction placeholders, enter a numerator and a denominator.

5 Insert symbols such as a multiplication, division, or not-equal sign from the Symbols gallery, as needed.

6 Type numbers, variables, and insert other symbols as desired to complete the equation.

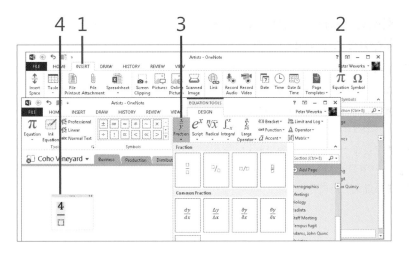

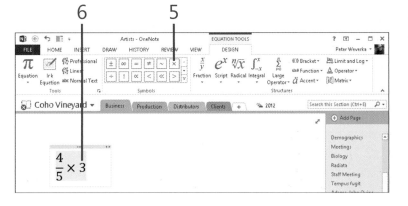

> **TRY THIS** In the Equation Tools | Design contextual tab, click Equation and choose a common equation on the gallery as a starting point for constructing your equation. You can also do this on the Insert tab by opening the gallery on the Equation button.

Recording audio and video notes

If your computer is equipped with audio-recording and video-recording capability, you can record audio and video notes and play back the recordings on the Audio & Video Playback tab of OneNote 2013.

OneNote stores audio recordings as .wma files; it stores video recordings as .wmv files. The icons for .wma and .wmv files appear in notes when you record audio and video notes.

Record an audio or video note

1 Click in a note and then, on the ribbon, click the Insert tab.

2 In the Recording group, click either Record Audio or Record Video and make your recording.

3 When you finish recording, on the Audio & Video | Recording contextual tab, click Stop.

> **TIP** You can click the Pause button to suspend the recording. Any notes you type during the recording are linked to the recording.

> **TRY THIS** The Audio & Video | Playback contextual tab also offers a Record Audio and a Record Video button. Click one of these buttons to record another audio or video note on the page.

Playing back audio and video notes

After you've recorded audio or video on a note, you can play back the recording. The Audio & Video | Playback contextual tab offers commands for playing, pausing, stopping, rewinding, and fast-forwarding an audio or video recording.

Play back audio or video notes

1 Click the note that contains the audio or video recording.

2 On the ribbon, click the Audio & Video | Playback contextual tab.

3 In the Playback group, click Play. You can also play a recording by double-clicking its icon.

4 Click Pause to suspend the recording temporarily.

5 Click the Play button next to a paragraph or note to play one portion of the recording (the portion you made while writing the note).

> **TIP** OneNote links recordings to notes that you take while a recording is being made or played back, and you can click these playback links to revisit different parts of a recording. To play back your supervisor's speech at a staff meeting, for example, you can select the note that you wrote while your supervisor spoke and then click the playback link attached to the note. In this way, you can write notes about meetings and events, and use your notes as a means to return to the parts of meetings and events that you recorded.

Putting a table in a note

For presenting information, it's hard to beat a table. Because the data in a table is arranged in columns and rows, a table gives you a concise picture of data. You can compare and contrast the numbers in a table and tell what's what. You can see trends and tell at a glance who or what is performing well or lagging behind.

However, creating a table can be a chore. You need the correct number of columns and rows to hold the data. Columns must be the right width to fully display the data. You need to align the numbers and text to make the data speak to the reader.

Microsoft OneNote 2013 offers all kinds of tools on the Table Tools Layout tab to help you make your tables just-so. In this section, you'll explore how to create a table in a note, insert and delete columns and rows, and select parts of a table so you can format the table's various parts. You also see how to sort table data, manage table borders, change column widths, and align the text.

For fans of Microsoft Excel 2013, this section also explores how to create an Excel spreadsheet in OneNote and turn a OneNote table into an Excel spreadsheet.

In this section:

- Creating a table
- Inserting and deleting columns and rows
- Selecting parts of a table
- Sorting data in a table
- Hiding or displaying table borders
- Changing the width of columns
- Aligning text in tables
- Creating an Excel spreadsheet in a note
- Converting a table into an Excel spreadsheet

Creating a table

A table is composed of columns and rows. The columns and rows intersect to form cells. It's within these cells that you enter data. You can make a table a part of a note or make it a note unto itself. Make a table a part of a note, for example, to introduce the table with a descriptive sentence or two.

After you construct the table, you can modify it to your liking. For example, you can format the text in different ways and change the size and color of the table.

Create a table

1 Click in a note (to insert a table in a note) or click the page (to create a stand-alone table in a new note).

2 On the ribbon, click the Insert tab.

3 Click the Table button.

4 Use one of these techniques to tell OneNote how many columns and rows you want:

- Click in the table grid. For example, to create a table that has five columns and five rows (as shown in the illustration), click in the square that is five columns across and five rows down.

- Click Insert Table. In the Insert Table dialog box that opens, enter the number of columns and rows, and click OK.

(continued on next page)

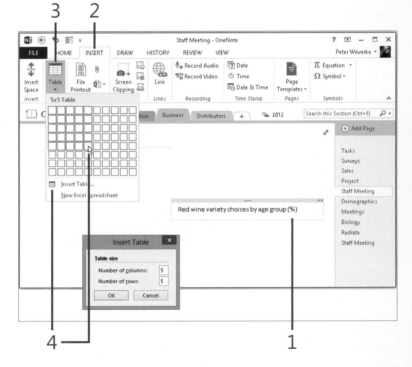

Create a table *(continued)*

5 Enter text into the cells of the table (a cell is the place where a column and row intersect; each cell can hold one data item. Press Tab to move to the next cell.)

5

Red wine variety choices by age group (%):

Age	Barbera	Cabernet	Chablis	Malbec
21-30	1	8	33	1
31-40	1	15	22	1
41-50	1	18	20	1
50+	2	25	14	1

TRY THIS   A quick way to create a table is to type the first table entry and then press Tab. OneNote creates a simple one-row, two-column table. To add columns to this table, press Tab with the cursor in the rightmost column. After you add the columns, you can add rows by placing the cursor in the last row, rightmost column and then pressing Enter.

TIP   To delete the data in a table cell, select the data and press the Delete key. To delete the contents of several adjacent cells, drag over the cells to select them, and press Delete.

TIP   To make room in a note for a table title, click to the left of the first entry in the table and press Enter. For example, if the first entry (the entry in column 1, row 1) is the word Age, click to the left of the letter A and press Enter. OneNote adds space at the top of the note for a title or other text.

Inserting and deleting columns and rows

Unless you are lucky or clever enough to choose the right number of columns and rows for your table when you create it, you need to add or delete columns and rows as you construct your table. On the Table Tools | Layout tab, OneNote offers commands to do just that.

Insert a column or row

1 Click in the column or row adjacent to where you want to insert a new column or row.

- To insert a column, click anywhere in an existing column to the left or right of the column that you want to insert.

- To insert a row, click anywhere in an existing row above or below the row that you want to insert.

2 On the ribbon, click the Table Tools | Layout contextual tab.

3 In the Insert group, click one of the Insert buttons:

- Click Insert Left (or press Ctrl+Alt+E) or Insert Right (or press Ctrl+Alt+R) to insert a column.

- Click Insert Above or Insert Below (or press Ctrl+Enter) to insert a row.

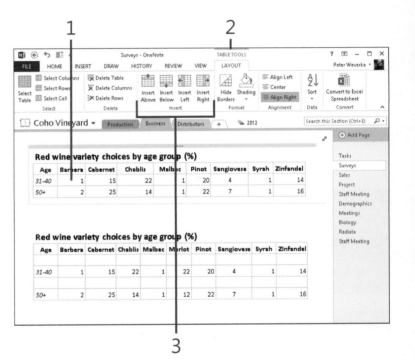

✓ **TIP** You can insert more than one column or row at a time by selecting cells in more than one column or row before clicking an Insert button. For example, to insert two columns, drag the mouse to select any adjacent cells in two existing columns and then click the Insert Left or Insert Right button.

Delete a column or row

1 Click in the column or row that you want to delete.

2 On the ribbon, click the Table Tools | Layout contextual tab.

3 In the Delete group, click Delete Columns or Delete Rows. The selected columns or rows immediately disappear, along with their data.

TIP To delete more than one column or row at a time, select the columns or rows (by dragging over two or more cells in the same column or row and then clicking a Select button) and then click a Delete button.

TRY THIS Need to delete an entire table, maybe to start all over? Click anywhere in the table, click Layout, and then click Delete Table. (Click the Undo button immediately if you regret deleting your table.)

Selecting parts of a table

Before you can format part of a table, delete a column or row, or add a column or row, you must select part of the table. For example, to bold text in the first row, select the first row and click the Bold button on the Home tab (or press Ctrl+B).

After you select a part of a table, it is highlighted. Formatting commands that you apply while part of a table is highlighted apply to all highlighted parts.

Select a cell, column, row, or table

1 Click the part of the table that you want to select. For example, to select a column or row, click anywhere in the column or row.

2 On the ribbon, click the Table Tools | Layout contextual tab.

3 In the Select group, click Select Table, Select Columns, Select Rows, or Select Cell.

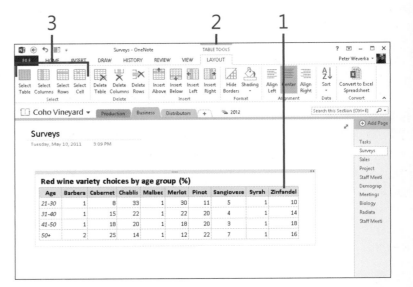

> ✓ **TIP**   You can select more than one column or row by dragging across cells in more than one column or row before clicking a Select button. For example, drag over two cells in adjacent columns and then click Select Columns to select both columns.

Sorting data in a table

Sorting a table means to rearrange the data in one column so that it falls in alphabetical or numerical order. Sorting makes the information in a table easier to understand. For example, finding a name in a long list is easier when the list has been sorted alphabetically. In a table of sales figures, comparing the figures is easier when they are sorted from largest to smallest or smallest to largest.

You can sort table data in ascending or descending order:

- **Sort Ascending** Arranges text in alphabetical order from A to Z, and numbers from smallest to largest.

- **Sort Descending** Arranges text from Z to A, and numbers from largest to smallest.

Sort table data

1 Click in the column that you want to use to sort the table (don't select the column).

2 On the ribbon, click the Table Tools | Layout contextual tab.

3 Click the Sort button and choose Sort Ascending or Sort Descending.

> **TIP** By default, OneNote does not include the header row in sort operations (the header row is the topmost row in the table that identifies what is in the columns below). If your table doesn't have a header row, click the Sort button, and in the drop-down list, clear the Header Row item before choosing a Sort command.

> **TIP** You can sort some of the rows within a table by selecting the rows, clicking the Sort button, and choosing Sort Selected Rows. The Sort dialog box opens. Choose a column by which to sort, the Ascending or Descending option, and then click OK.

Hiding or displaying table borders

Table borders are the lines in a table that mark where the rows and columns are. Borders are convenient for entering data in a table. You can see clearly where to enter each data item. But sometimes a table looks better without the borders.

The Hide Borders button acts like a toggle, making it easy for you to hide or display table borders as needed.

Hide or display table borders

1 Click anywhere in the table.

2 On the ribbon, click the Table Tools | Layout contextual tab.

3 In the Format group, click Hide Borders.

If borders are currently displayed, they are hidden. To redisplay them, click in the table and then click the Hide Borders button again.

Red wine variety choices by age group (%)

Age	Barbera	Cabernet	Chablis	Malbec	Merlot	Pinot	Sangiovese	Syrah	Zinfandel
21-30	1	8	33	1	30	11	5	1	10
31-40	1	15	22	1	22	20	4	1	14
41-50	1	18	20	1	18	20	3	1	18
50+	2	25	14	1	12	22	7	1	16

 TIP Hide table borders to prevent them from being printed when you print a page.

Changing the width of columns

To make data fit more snugly in a table, it's sometimes necessary to change the width of columns and make them narrower or wider. You can do that by dragging column borders.

The only way to change the height of rows is to enlarge the text in a table. OneNote makes each row tall enough to accommodate its tallest entry. By enlarging the text, you also enlarge the row height.

Change the width of a column

1 Hover the pointer over the right border of the column whose width you want to change.

2 When the two-headed arrow cursor appears, drag to the left (to narrow the column) or the right (to widen it).

SEE ALSO To learn how to display borders in a table, see "Hiding or displaying table borders" on page 106.

Aligning text in tables

Align text in a table in different ways to make the table easier to read and understand. Typically, numbers are right-aligned so that the decimal points line up under one another and the numbers are easier to compare. Labels are typically center-aligned or left-aligned. OneNote provides alignment buttons on the Table Tools | Layout contextual tab for aligning text.

Left-align, center, or right-align text

1 Select the rows, columns, or cells that contain the data you want to realign; or, select the entire table.

2 On the ribbon, click the Table Tools | Layout contextual tab.

3 In the Alignment group, click Align Left, Center, or Align Right.

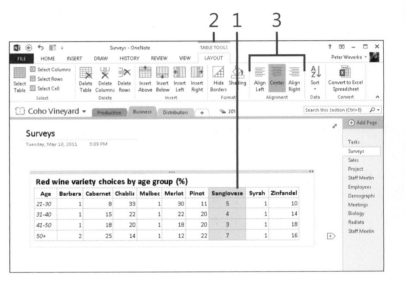

TIP Press Ctrl+R to right-align data in cells; press Ctrl+L to left-align data.

TIP You can also align data in tables by selecting cells with the text, going to the Home tab, clicking the Paragraph Alignment button, and choosing Align Left, Center, or Align Right.

SEE ALSO To learn how to select cells, columns, rows, or an entire table, read "Selecting parts of a table" on page 104.

Creating an Excel spreadsheet in a note

Microsoft Excel 2013 is a spreadsheet program for recording and analyzing data. Chances are, when you installed OneNote 2013 on your computer, you also installed Excel.

OneNote gives you the ability to create an Excel spreadsheet (assuming Excel is installed on your computer). The Excel spreadsheet you create is embedded in your OneNote notebook. In computer lingo, embedding is when data from one type of program (Excel in this case) is stored in a file normally associated with another type of program (OneNote in this case).

When you want to edit your spreadsheet, you click the Edit button to launch Excel. Now, you can take advantage of all the Excel commands for recording and analyzing data.

Using Excel's tools, you can add calculations and formulas to the table to manipulate its data. You can also filter, consolidate, and graph data—tasks you can't do in OneNote. What's more, Excel offers many more opportunities for formatting and decorating tables than does OneNote.

Create an Excel spreadsheet in a note

1 On the ribbon, click the Insert tab.

2 In the Files group, click Spreadsheet.

3 Choose New Excel Spreadsheet.

4 Click Edit to open Excel.

(continued on next page)

Create an Excel spreadsheet in a note *(continued)*

5 Enter and format data in Excel.

6 Click Save (or press Ctrl+S) to save your Excel data.

7 Click Close in Excel to return to OneNote.

You'll notice that an embedded Excel spreadsheet has a thicker border than a OneNote table, and that it bears the notation, Table–Spreadsheet.

TIP You can also insert an Excel spreadsheet by clicking Insert, clicking Table, and in the menu that appears, choosing New Excel Spreadsheet.

Edit an Excel spreadsheet in a note

1 Move the pointer over the embedded Excel spreadsheet.

2 Click the Edit button.

3 Edit your Excel data.

4 Click the Save button.

5 Click Close.

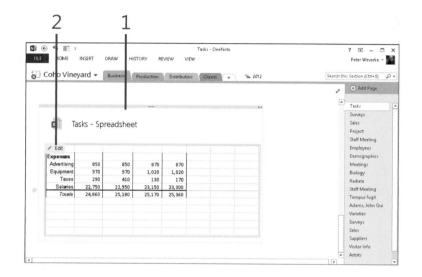

SEE ALSO To learn how to convert a table you already created into an Excel spreadsheet, read "Converting a table into an Excel spreadsheet" on page 112.

Converting a table into an Excel spreadsheet

You can convert a table into an Excel worksheet when you want to use Excel 2013 to perform sophisticated data analysis on the data in the table. For example, after converting a OneNote table to an Excel worksheet, you can create a chart or PivotTable from the data.

Converting the table turns it into an embedded Excel spreadsheet. By clicking the Edit button in the converted table, you can open your table in Excel and use Excel commands for data analysis.

The data in the table is stored in your OneNote file, not in an Excel spreadsheet.

Convert a table into an Excel spreadsheet

1 Click anywhere in the OneNote table.

You'll notice that a OneNote table has a thin border, whereas an embedded Excel spreadsheet has a thicker border and bears the notation, Table–Spreadsheet.

2 On the ribbon, click the Table Tools | Layout contextual tab.

3 Click Convert To Excel Spreadsheet.

The table is converted to an embedded Excel spreadsheet.

Red wine variety choices by age group (%)

Age	Barbera	Cabernet	Chablis	Malbec	Merlot	Pinot	Sangiovese	Syrah	Zinfandel
21-30	1	8	33	1	30	11	5	1	10
31-40	1	15	22	1	22	20	4	1	14
41-50	1	18	20	1	18	20	3	1	18
50+	2	25	14	1	12	22	7	1	16

SEE ALSO To learn how to create an Excel spreadsheet from within OneNote, read "Creating an Excel spreadsheet in a note" on page 109.

Linking your notes

7

Microsoft OneNote 2013 offers all kinds of opportunities for linking. You can link to other sections and pages in a notebook, to other notebooks, to webpages, and to files. With the Linked Notes feature, you can even tell OneNote to link automatically to Microsoft Word documents, Microsoft PowerPoint presentations, webpages, and other OneNote pages as you take notes on them.

A link is a shortcut from one place to another. Rather than go to the trouble of opening a document in Word when you need it, you can create a link to the document in OneNote and open the Word document simply by clicking the link. Create links as a way to navigate from OneNote to webpages, files, and other OneNote pages.

Links help you integrate OneNote with your other work.

In this section:

- Linking to other places in OneNote
- Linking to another notebook
- Linking to a place in the same notebook
- Creating a link to a webpage
- Creating a link to a file
- Editing links
- Taking linked notes
- Viewing files or pages linked to notes

Linking to other places in OneNote

You can create a link to a notebook, section, page, or note so that you can click the link and instantly display it. You can link to a place in another notebook or the same notebook. Links offer a convenient way to go from place to place within OneNote 2013. They also present an opportunity to organize your notes. For example, you can create a table of contents page with links to other sections and pages in the same or different notebook, and use that page to jump to important information quickly.

You can also create links to webpages. These links offer an easy way to open webpages quickly and display them in your browser. In addition, you can create links to files such as Word documents, PowerPoint presentations, Excel worksheets, graphics, and audio and video files.

Links are displayed as blue, underlined text. When you move the pointer over a link, a ScreenTip appears and the pointer turns into a hand. The ScreenTip shows you the file path to the notebook, section, page, or note you will display by clicking the link.

When you click a link, the linked item appears. Links can direct you to a notebook, section, page, note, webpage, or file. After you click a link, you can return to your original place in OneNote by clicking the Back button on the Quick Access Toolbar (or by pressing Alt+Left Arrow). Clicking the Back button is similar to returning to a previous page in a web browser.

The easiest way to link to another place in OneNote is to right-click the item that you want the link to point to and then, on the shortcut menu that appears, choose Copy Link To and paste the link into a note. The text of the pasted link shows the name of the the linked notebook, section, or page, or in the case of a note, some of the note's text. You can change the link text after pasting it if you want.

You can also edit a link to change the destination item to which it is directed, or remove a link when you don't need it anymore.

Click the Back button to return from a link.

Click a link to go to another notebook, section, page, or note.

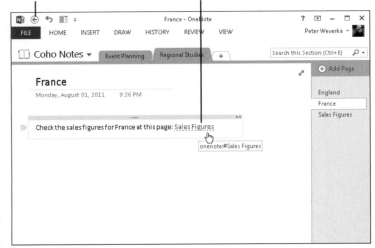

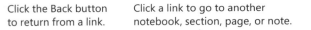

SEE ALSO To learn to how link to various other items, read the following tasks: "Linking to another notebook" on page 115; "Linking to a place in the same notebook" on page 117; "Creating a link to a webpage" on page 119; and "Creating a link to a file" on page 120.

Linking to another notebook

You can create a link to another OneNote 2013 notebook so that you can click the link and instantly visit the other notebook. Linking to another notebook is a convenient way to go precisely where you want to go in the other notebook, because you can link to a specific section, page, or note.

After the link is created, all you have to do is click the link to open the other notebook. What happens when you click the link depends on whether the other notebook is open and whether your link goes to a specific page, section, or note:

- **Link to a closed notebook** The notebook opens to the first section, first page.

- **Link to an open notebook** The notebook opens to whatever page is currently open.

- **Link to a specific place (whether the notebook is open or closed)** The notebook opens to that section, page, or note.

You can create a link to another notebook in one of two ways: by right-clicking the target of the link and pasting the link into your note, or by using the Link dialog box.

Link to another notebook by right-clicking

1 Open the notebook to which you want to link. In the notebook in which you want to insert the link, in the Notebooks pane, right-click the destination notebook or section in the other notebook.

2 On the shortcut menu that appears, click Copy Link To Notebook or Copy Link To Section.

3 Go to the page where you want to paste the link.

4 Click on a page.

5 On the ribbon, click the Home tab.

6 In the Clipboard group, click Paste. The link is created. To activate the link, click it.

> → **TRY THIS** Click the Back button (on the Quick Access Toolbar) after you click a link. Clicking the Back button returns you to the page where the link is located.

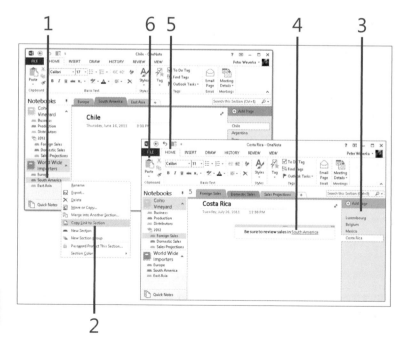

Link to another notebook by using the Link dialog box

1 Make sure that the notebook to which you want to link is open.

2 Click on a OneNote page where you want to place the link. You can select text to use as the link if you want.

3 On the ribbon, click the Insert tab.

4 In the links group, click Link.

5 In the Link dialog box, in the Or Pick A Location In OneNote list box, select the notebook to which you want to link.

You can select a section or page in the notebook to link directly to it. (To display the pages in a section, click the plus sign adjacent to the section name.)

6 Click OK. The link is created. To activate the link, click it.

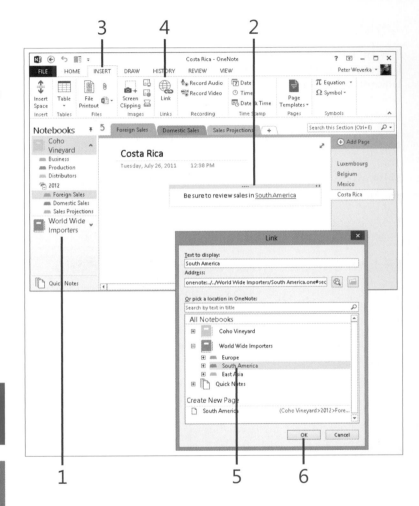

TIP You can create your own link text by selecting the text that you want to use as the link before Step 5. Press Ctrl+K to make the text a hyperlink and then paste the link you copied.

CAUTION Before you try to link to another notebook by using the Link dialog box, open the other notebook. The other notebook must be open for its name to appear in the Link dialog box.

SEE ALSO To learn how to edit, rewrite, and remove a link, read "Editing links" on page 121.

Linking to a place in the same notebook

Linking to different places in the same OneNote 2013 notebook is a great way to get from place to place quickly. These links present an opportunity to organize your notes.

For example, you can create a page with links to other sections or pages in a notebook and use this page to quickly go to where important information is stored. You can also link to a note, which is handy if you need to go to a note on a page with many notes. You can link to a specific paragraph in a note, as well.

Link to a place in the same notebook by right-clicking

1 Right-click the section tab, page tab, or note to which you want to link.

2 On the shortcut menu that appears, click Copy Link To Section, Copy Link To Page, or Copy Link To Paragraph.

3 Click on a page where you want the link to appear.

4 On the ribbon, click the Home tab.

5 In the Clipboard group, click Paste. The link is created. To activate the link, click it.

> **TIP** OneNote offers a shortcut for linking to a page in the currently open notebook: Type two left square brackets ([[), the page's name, and two right square brackets (]]). For example, typing [[Compounds]] creates a link named "Compounds"; clicking this link opens the Compounds page. If OneNote can't find a page with the name you entered, it searches other open notebooks for the page, and if OneNote can't find the page in any open notebooks, it creates a new page and gives this page the name you entered. This is an easy way to not only create a new page, but to create a link to it at the same time.

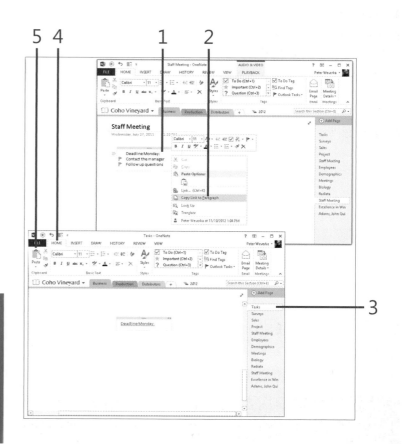

Link to a place in the same notebook by using the Link dialog box

1 Click on a OneNote page where you want to place the link. You can select text to use as the link if you want.

2 On the ribbon, click the Insert tab.

3 In the Link group, click Link.

4 In the Link dialog box, in the Or Pick A Location In OneNote list box, select the notebook to which you want to link. (To display the pages in a section, click the plus sign in front of the section name.)

5 Click OK. The link is created. To activate the link, click it.

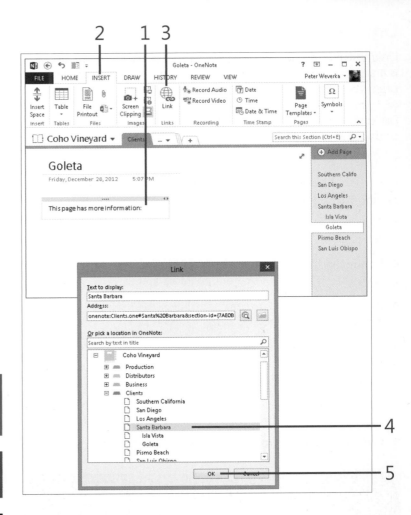

 TIP You can create your own link text by selecting the text that you want to use as the link before Step 4. Press Ctrl+K to make the text a hyperlink and then paste the link you copied.

SEE ALSO To learn how to edit, rewrite, and remove a link, read "Editing links" on page 121.

TRY THIS Move the pointer over a link. A ScreenTip shows you the path to the link's location. Click the link. Then, click the Back button on the Quick Access Toolbar to return to the page where the link is located.

Creating a link to a webpage

Create a link to a webpage so that you can click the link and immediately open the webpage in your browser. Rather than open your browser and then go to a webpage, you can simply click the link in your OneNote 2013 notebook and conveniently go to the webpage straightaway.

To create a link to a webpage, you need to know the address of the webpage to which the link will go. The easiest way to obtain this is to go to the webpage and copy the address from your browser's address bar. You can paste it into the Link dialog box.

When you move the pointer over a link to a webpage, a Screen-Tip appears and shows you the webpage address.

Create a link to a webpage

1 Click on a OneNote page where you want to place the link. You can select text to use as the link if you want.

2 On the ribbon, click the Insert tab.

3 In the Links group, click Link.

4 In the Link dialog box, to the right of the Address text box, click the Browse The Web button. Your web browser opens.

5 In your web browser, go to the webpage to which you want to link.

6 On the web browser's address bar, right-click the web address and, on the shortcut menus that appears, choose Copy.

7 Back in the Link dialog box, right-click in the Address box to open a shortcut menu and then click Paste.

8 Click OK. The link is created. To activate the link, click it.

 SEE ALSO To learn how to take notes on a webpage as you view it, read "Taking linked notes" on page 123.

SEE ALSO To learn how to insert a screen clipping (a picture of part of a webpage, document, or other item on your computer screen) and insert it in a note, read "Take a screen clipping" on page 92.

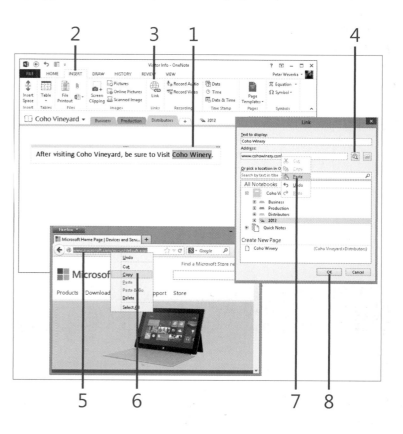

Creating a link to a file

You can create a link to a file in OneNote 2013, making it possible to open the file by clicking its link. For example, clicking a link to a Word document opens the document in Word. You can link to any file, not just Microsoft Office files.

A file link is an opportunity for you to quickly refer to a file or to trade information between a note and a file. All you have to do is click the link to examine the file.

When you move the pointer over a file link, a ScreenTip appears with the path to the file and the file's name.

Create a link to a file

1 Click on a OneNote page where you want to place the link. You can select text to use as the link if you want.

2 On the ribbon, click the Insert tab.

3 In the Link group, click Link.

4 In the Links dialog box, to the right of the Address text box, click the Browse For File button.

5 In the Link To File dialog box, browse to the file to which you want to link, select the file, and then click OK.

6 Click OK. The link is created. To activate the link, click it.

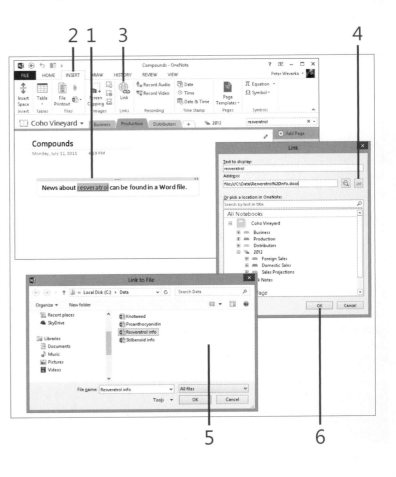

> ⚠️ **CAUTION** A file link is broken if the target file is deleted or moved. When you click a broken link, the Unable To Open File dialog box appears. You can edit the link to fix it so that it points to the right location of the file, or you can remove the link altogether.

> 🔍 **SEE ALSO** To learn how to attach the contents of a file to a note, or to insert a file's contents into a note, read "Attaching a file or copying a file's contents to a note" on page 84.

Editing links

Sometimes a link needs editing. For example, the target of the link changes and the link needs to go to a different notebook, file, or webpage. Or, the text that forms the link needs a rewrite or needs to be removed altogether.

OneNote offers the Link dialog box for editing links. In this dialog box, you can rewrite link text or direct the link to a different target. You can also remove a link without having to open the Link dialog box.

Edit a link

1 Right-click the link that you want to edit. (Link text is normally blue and underlined.)

2 On the shortcut menu that appears, click Edit Link.

3 In the Link dialog box, rewrite the link text in the Text To Display box if you want.

4 Choose a different location for the link:

- To link to a different webpage, click the Browse The Web button.

- To link to a different target file, click the Browse For File button.

- Choose a different page, section, or notebook in the All Note-books list.

5 Click OK.

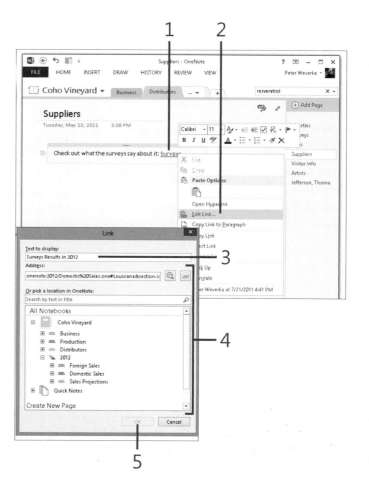

> ✅ **TIP** To format the text that forms a link, right-click the link and then, on the shortcut menu that appears, click Select Link. After the text is selected, on the Home tab, you can apply text formatting commands as you would to any other text in the note.

> ✅ **TIP** You can copy a link to other pages in your notebook. Right-click the link and then, on the shortcut menu that appears, click Copy Link. Then, paste the link on a different page.

Remove a link

1 Right-click a link to a webpage, file, or OneNote location. (Link text is blue and underlined.)

2 On the shortcut menu that appears, click Remove Link.

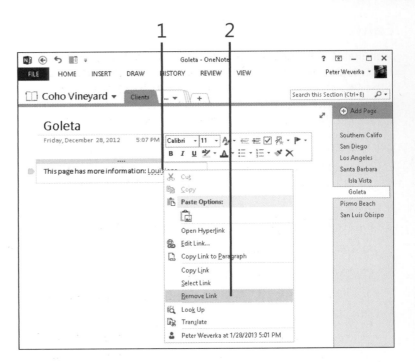

> ⚠ **CAUTION** After you remove a link, the text remains but the link is no longer active. To remove the text, select it and press Delete.

Taking linked notes

Linked notes are notes that are linked to a webpage, Word document, PowerPoint presentation, or OneNote 2013 page. After you click the Link Notes button, OneNote opens a docked window; notes you take in this window are automatically linked to the webpage, Word document, PowerPoint presentation, or OneNote page that is open on your screen.

Taking linked notes is a convenient way to refer to an item about which you took notes. All you have to do to open the item is click the Internet Explorer icon, Word icon, PowerPoint icon, or OneNote icon in the note. These icons appear to the left of paragraphs in linked notes.

You can start taking linked notes in one of two ways: from within OneNote or from within Word, PowerPoint, or Internet Explorer. When you finish taking linked notes, close the docked window.

Take linked notes starting in OneNote

1 On the ribbon, click the Review tab.

2 In the Notes group, click Linked Notes.

3 Select the OneNote page on which you want to take notes and click OK.

   A second OneNote window opens and docks to the right side of the screen. The page you selected appears in the docked window.

4 On the left side of the screen, display the OneNote page, Internet Explorer page, Word file, or PowerPoint file on which you want to take notes.

5 In the docked OneNote window, write notes regarding the file or page on display.

6 Change to other files or pages to take notes on them if you want.

7 When you finish taking notes, click Close in the docked window.

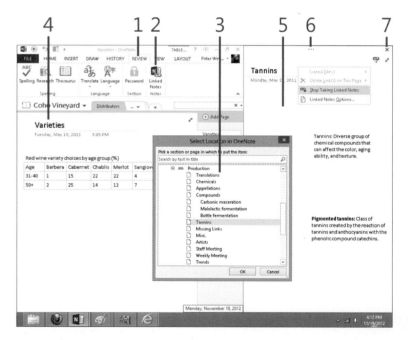

> **SEE ALSO** To learn how to create a link to a notebook, read, "Linking to other places in OneNote" on page 114.

Take linked notes starting in Word or PowerPoint

1 Display the Word document or PowerPoint presentation on which you want to take notes.

2 On the ribbon, click the Review tab.

3 In the OneNote group, click Linked Notes.

4 Select the OneNote page on which you want to take notes and click OK.

A OneNote window opens and docks to the right side of the screen so that you can take notes on the page you selected.

5 In the docked OneNote window, write notes regarding the document or presentation in the displayed in the window on the left.

6 When you finish taking notes, click Close in the docked window.

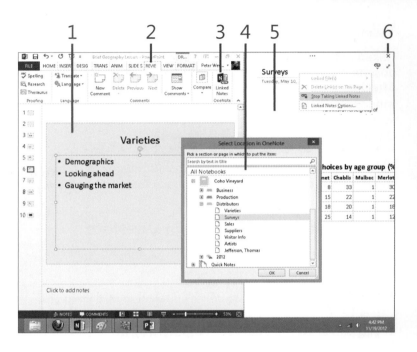

Viewing files or pages linked to notes

You can see when a OneNote 2013 page has links to Word documents, PowerPoint presentations, webpages, or other OneNote pages because the Linked Notes icon appears in the upper-right corner of the page.

By clicking a link icon on the left side of paragraphs, you can open files to which the paragraph is linked. You can review these files as you review your notes.

View files or webpages linked to notes

1 Open a page in OneNote on which linked notes were taken. (Look for the Linked Notes icon in the upper-right corner of the page.)

2 Hover the pointer over notes to see which notes are linked to files or webpages.

   As you move the pointer over a linked note, an icon appears to the left of the note.

3 Hover the pointer over an icon to see a file name or webpage thumbnail.

4 Click an icon to open the file or webpage to which a note is linked.

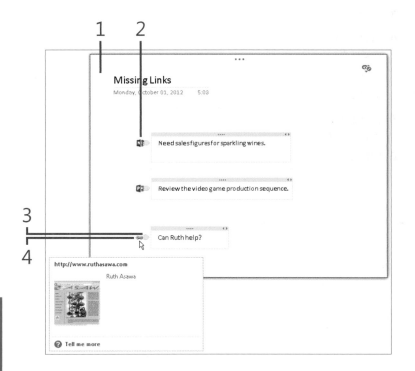

> **TIP** Click the Link icon at the top of a page with linked notes and choose Delete Link(s) On This Page to see a submenu with the names of all links on the page. Select a link to delete it and click OK; select Delete All Links On This Page to delete all the links. Removing links does not remove the note text associated with them. You can also delete a link by right-clicking its icon and choosing Remove Link.

> **SEE ALSO** To edit, rewrite, and remove a link that is not working, read "Editing links" on page 121.

Making OneNote easier to use

Microsoft OneNote 2013 presents many opportunities for rearranging and changing the screen so that you can get your work done faster and easier.

When you need more room in the page window to write and read notes, you can minimize the Notebooks pane, pages tabs, and the ribbon. You can change views, as well. OneNote 2013 offers Full Page view for reading and editing notes and Normal view for organizing and formatting notes.

When you're taking notes from a web browser or application, consider docking OneNote to the desktop. Docking entails moving the OneNote screen to the right side of the monitor window, making it possible for you to write notes and still see other applications.

To quickly switch between different pages, open a second (or third or fourth) OneNote window. You can jump from window to window by clicking the OneNote button on the Windows taskbar and making a page selection.

OneNote also offers the standard zoom-in and zoom-out commands to make reading easier. These commands are found on the View tab of the ribbon.

In this section:

- Collapsing and expanding the Note-books pane and page tabs
- Pinning and collapsing the ribbon
- Changing screen views
- Docking OneNote to the desktop
- Opening another OneNote window
- Zooming in and out

Collapsing and expanding the Notebooks pane and page tabs

In Normal View, the Notebooks pane (on the left side of the screen) and page tabs (on the right side) are fully displayed. The Notebooks pane lists the names of open notebooks, and within each notebook, the names of sections and section groups. The page tabs show you the names of pages and subpages in the section you are viewing. Use the Notebooks pane and page tabs to get from place to place in OneNote 2013.

To make more room in the page window for writing and reading notes, you can collapse (hide) the Notebooks pane and page tabs (making them narrower). And when you want to see the Notebooks pane and page tabs again, you can expand (display) them.

Collapse and expand the Notebooks pane

1 Move the pointer over the border between the Notebooks pane and the page window. When you see the double-headed arrow, drag the border to the right to widen the Notebook pane so that you can view its contents more easily.

2 Click the Unpin Notebook Pane From Side button (located at the top of the Notebooks pane) to widen the page and be able to read more notes. Click the Show Notebooks button to choose a notebook to view when the Notebooks pane is hidden.

(continued on next page)

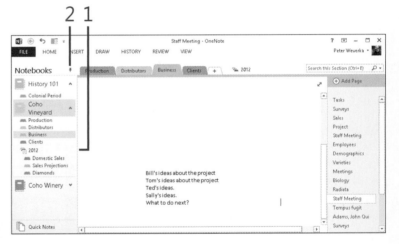

> **SEE ALSO** Hide the page tabs and the Notebooks pane quickly by changing to Full Page view. To learn how to switch between Normal view and Full Page view, read "Changing screen views" on page 133.

> **TIP** If you only work with one notebook, consider hiding the Notebooks pane altogether. On the ribbon, click File to display the Backstage view, click the Options tab, and then, in the OneNote Options dialog box, choose Display and clear the Navigation Bar Appears On Left check box. Click OK to save the settings and close the dialog box.

Collapse and expand the Notebooks
pane *(continued)*

4   3

3 Click the Show Notebooks button to choose a notebook to view when the Notebooks pane is hidden.

4 From the menu that appears, choose a notebook. The Notebooks pane collapses again after you make your choice.

5 Double-click the Show Notebooks button to redisplay the Notebooks pane.

Collapse and expand the page tabs

1 Move the pointer over the border between the page tabs and the page window. When you see the double-headed arrow, drag the border to the left to widen the page tabs so you can view the page names more easily.

2 Drag the border to the right to narrow the page tabs.

✓ **TIP** Press Ctrl+Shift+[to widen the page tabs; press Ctrl+Shift+] to narrow them. Keep pressing a keyboard shortcut until the page tabs are the size you want.

Showing and collapsing the ribbon

The ribbon is the assortment of buttons and commands that appears along the top of the OneNote 2013 window when you click a tab. When you need to focus on reading notes, consider collapsing the ribbon to hide it temporarily. With the ribbon collapsed, there is more room for reading notes.

When the ribbon is collapsed, you can still access the buttons and other commands on a tab by clicking a tab name. The tab you select displays in full. After you perform an action by using one of the tools on the tab, the ribbon collapses again.

Collapse the ribbon

1 On the right end of the ribbon, click the Collapse button (or press Ctrl+F1) to collapse and hide the ribbon.

The ribbon disappears, save for the tab names, which display near the top of the window.

2 Click a tab name.

The tab and its tools and commands appear.

3 Click a button on the tab.

In most cases, the ribbon remains on the screen so that you can click another button on the tab if you need to.

4 Click on the page.

The ribbon collapses from view again.

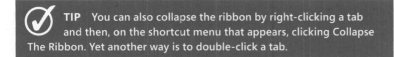

TIP You can also collapse the ribbon by right-clicking a tab and then, on the shortcut menu that appears, clicking Collapse The Ribbon. Yet another way is to double-click a tab.

SEE ALSO Another way to collapse the ribbon is to switch to Full Page view. See "Changing screen views" on page 133 to learn how to switch between Normal view and Full Page view.

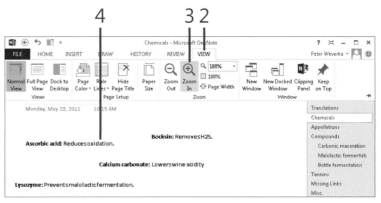

Show the ribbon

1 With the ribbon collapsed, click the Ribbon Display Options button.

2 On the menu that appears, click Show Tabs And Ribbons.

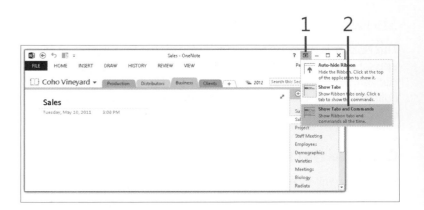

SEE ALSO   To learn how to customize the ribbon by adding or removing commands, read "Adding or removing commands from a ribbon group" on page 244.

TIP   OneNote also offers these techniques for showing the ribbon:

- Click a tab and then deselect the Pin The Ribbon button
- Press Ctrl+F1
- Double-click a tab

Changing screen views

OneNote 2013 offers three views in which you can choose to work. In Full Page view, the Notebooks pane and page tabs do not appear. In Normal view, you can see the Notebooks pane and page tabs. Normal view is the best view for writing, editing, and organizing notes; Full Page view is best for reading notes comfortably.

OneNote also offers Docked view, which you can use to view a webpage or document while taking notes in OneNote.

Change your view of the screen

1 Click the Full Page View button.

   The ribbon, Notebooks pane, and page tabs disappear from view.

2 At the top of the window, click the Ribbon button (the three dots) to display the ribbon.

3 Click the View tab.

4 In the Views group, click Normal View to return to Normal view.

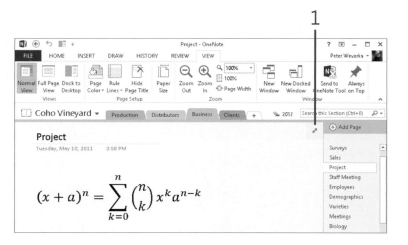

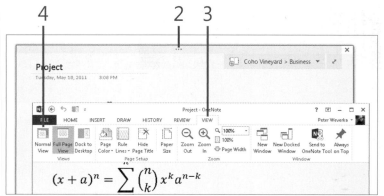

TIP The Normal View and Full Page View buttons are both toggles. This means that you can click either button to switch back and forth between Normal and Full Page views. The Full Page View button and F11 are also toggles that you can use to switch back and forth between views.

SEE ALSO To learn how to hide and display the Notebooks pane and page tabs in Normal view, read "Collapsing and expanding the Notebooks pane and page tabs" on page 128.

Docking OneNote to the desktop

Docking OneNote 2013 to the desktop means to shunt OneNote to the right side of the screen where it is out of the way but can still be used for taking and reading notes. For example, you might want to dock OneNote when you are taking notes from a browser window or file.

You can change the width of the OneNote screen after it is docked by dragging its left side. When docked, OneNote presents an abridged version of the ribbon with only three tabs: Home, Draw, and View. To display the ribbon, click the Ribbon button located at the top of the docked OneNote window.

Dock and undock OneNote to the desktop

1 On the Quick Access Toolbar in the OneNote window, click the Dock To Desktop button.

2 Move the pointer over the left edge of the docked window. When you see the double-headed arrow, drag to the left or right to change the size of the docked OneNote window.

3 To undock OneNote, in the upper-right corner, click the Normal View button.

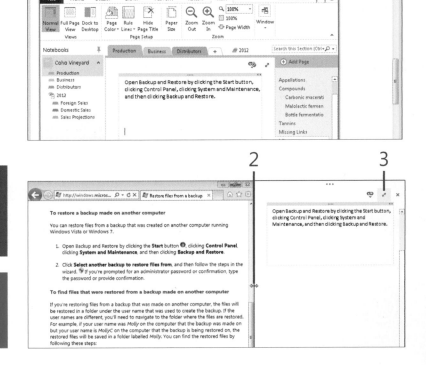

> **SEE ALSO** To learn how you can take notes in a docked OneNote window and have OneNote automatically link the notes you take to a webpage, Microsoft Word document, Microsoft PowerPoint presentation, or OneNote page that is open on the screen, read "Taking linked notes" on page 123.

> **TIP** Use these alternative techniques to dock OneNote: Click the Dock To Desktop button on the View tab, or press Ctrl+Alt+D. To undock OneNote, you can also click the Normal View button or press Ctrl+Alt+D.

Opening another OneNote window

You can open another OneNote 2013 window when you want to examine notes on different pages at the same time. You can place the other window wherever you like. You can also open another window and dock it to the desktop.

To switch between open OneNote windows, use the Windows taskbar.

Open another OneNote window

1 On the ribbon, click the View tab.

2 In the Window group, click New Window.

3 In the new window, in the page tabs, click a different page.

4 On the Windows taskbar, hover the pointer over the OneNote button to see thumbnails of open OneNote windows.

5 Click the thumbnail of the OneNote window to which you want to switch.

6 When you finish with a particular OneNote window, click its Close button to close the window.

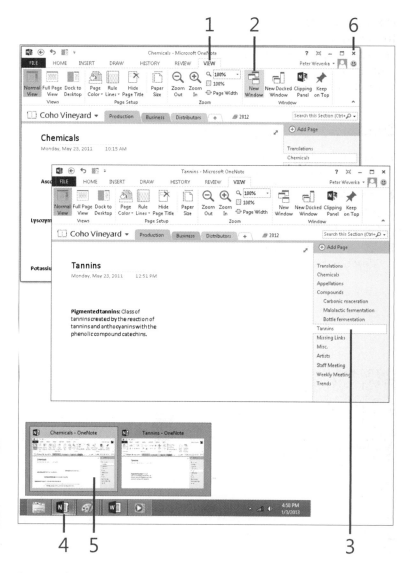

⊘ **TIP** To keep a OneNote window (or *the* OneNote window, if only one window is open) on top of all other open windows, on the View tab, click the Always On Top button .

⊘ **TIP** You can drag open windows on the screen. Drag them side by side to compare them, for example.

Zooming in and out

OneNote 2013 offers a number of Zoom buttons and controls on the View tab. You can use them to zoom in and out and get a better view of your work. Zoom in, for example, when drawing a note with precision; zoom out to see more notes on the page.

You can zoom in and out by a preset amount. You can also enter an exact percentage at which to zoom in or out.

Zoom in and out

1 On the ribbon, click the View tab.

2 In the Zoom group, click the Zoom drop-down arrow to open its menu and click a preset percentage to zoom in or out.

3 Click the 100% button to zoom to exactly 100%.

4 Click Zoom In to zoom in by 25% less.

5 Click Zoom Out to zoom out by 25% more.

6 Click Page Width to zoom in so that the width of the page is the same as the width of the window.

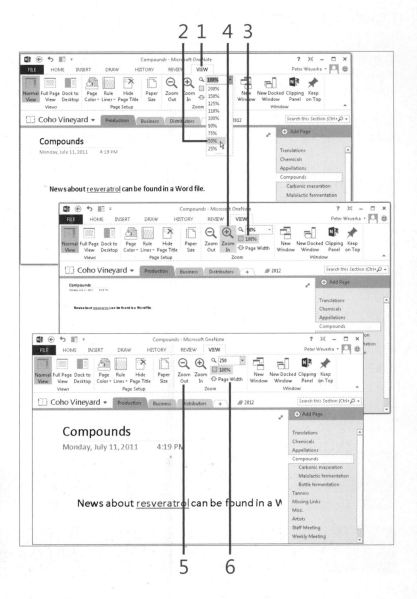

 TIP You can enter any percentage you want in the Zoom menu and press Enter to zoom to a percentage of your choice.

 TIP Click the Zoom In or Zoom Out multiple times to zoom in or out by preset amounts.

Using the spelling checker on your notes

9

If you intend to share notes with others, be sure to use the spelling checker on them to fix all misspellings. Microsoft OneNote 2013 offers a couple of different ways to check the spelling in notes. You can correct misspellings one at a time or run a spelling checker to review and correct all of them on a page.

If your notes include foreign language words, you can use the spelling checker on them, as well. OneNote 2013 also offers the AutoCorrect feature for correcting misspellings as you make them. You can add your own words to the list of words that are autocorrected. For that matter, you can trick the AutoCorrect feature into entering difficult-to-type words for you.

In this section:

- Running the spelling checker
- Customizing the spelling checker
- Using the spelling checker with foreign-language text
- Autocorrecting common misspellings

Running the spelling checker

Unless you opted to hide spelling errors in notes, you can see where spelling errors are because they are underlined in red. To fix spelling errors, you can either right-click misspelled words and correct them one at a time or run the spelling checker to examine the spelling on a single page.

The spelling checker occasionally flags a word that is correctly spelled. You can ignore these words or add them to the spelling dictionary. Adding a word to the spelling dictionary instructs OneNote that the word is legitimate and should no longer be considered a misspelling.

Correct misspellings one at a time

1   Right-click a misspelled word (a word underlined in red).

2   In the shortcut menu that appears, choose the correct spelling of the word from the suggestions.

3   Click or tap Ignore to disregard a word that OneNote presumes is incorrectly spelled but is actually a correct spelling.

4   Click Delete Repeated Word to remove a repeated word (the spelling checker flags identical words that appear one after the other).

5   Click Add To Dictionary to add a word to the dictionary so that OneNote no longer considers it a misspelling.

6   Click Spelling to open the Spelling task pane and run the spelling checker on the entire page.

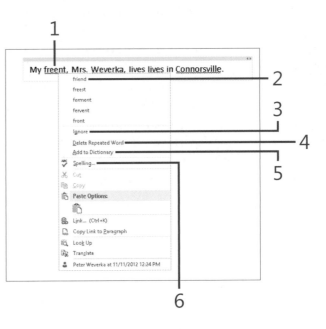

SEE ALSO   To learn how to hide or display the wavy red underlines that mark misspelled words, read "Customizing the spelling checker" on page 140.

TRY THIS   Type your last name in a note. If the spelling checker mistakes it for a misspelling, right-click your name, and then in the shortcut menu that appears, choose Add To Dictionary to add your name to the spelling dictionary so that it's never flagged again.

Run the spelling checker

1 Open the page on which you want to run the spelling checker.

2 On the ribbon, click the Review tab.

3 Click the Spelling button.

   The Spelling task pane opens.

4 From the Suggestions list, choose the correct spelling and then click Change.

5 Click tap Ignore to disregard a presumed misspelling.

6 Click Add to add a word to the dictionary that is correctly spelled but mistaken for a misspelling (adding the word to the dictionary deems it a correctly spelled word).

7 Click Delete to remove the second of two identical words (the Delete button appears in the Spelling task pane when the spelling checker encounters duplicate words).

8 Click the Close button to close the Spelling task pane.

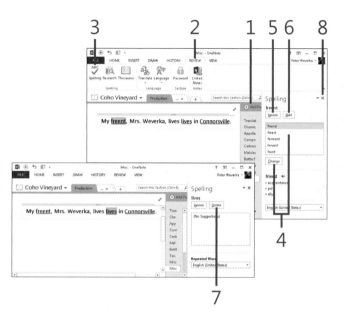

 TIP You can run a spelling check without going first to the Review tab and clicking the Spelling button by pressing F7.

⚠ **CAUTION** The spelling checker can't catch all misspellings. All it really does is call attention to words that aren't in its built-in dictionary. In the sentence "Nero diddled while Rome burned," for example, diddled is misspelled (the correct word is fiddled). But, because diddled is in its built-in dictionary, OneNote doesn't flag the misspelling. You have to rely on your proofreading skills as well as the spelling checker to catch all misspellings.

Customizing the spelling checker

OneNote 2013 offers many ways to customize the spelling checker to make it run more to your liking. For example, you can turn off the sometimes annoying wavy red lines that appear under misspelled words and choose whether to have the spelling checker examine uppercase words.

The options for customizing the spelling checker appear on the Proofing page of the OneNote Options dialog box.

OneNote spelling checker options

Option	Description
Ignore words in uppercase	Disregards any uppercase words on the presumption that they are acronyms.
Ignore words that contain numbers	Disregards words containing numbers.
Ignore Internet and file addresses	Disregards URLs and file addresses.
Flag repeated words	Flags any duplicate words.
Enforce accented uppercase in French	Flags uppercase letters in French words that should be accented (French-Canadian retains accents in uppercase words but standard French doesn't).
Suggest from main dictionary only	For spelling corrections, suggests words from the built-in dictionary, not dictionaries that you create or install.
Custom dictionaries	Click this button to open the Custom Dictionaries dialog box, in which you can edit the built-in dictionary (Custom.dic), choose the default dictionary for the spelling checker, create a dictionary, and install a dictionary.
French modes	When using the spelling checker on French words, determines how to handle traditional and new spellings.
Spanish modes	When using the spelling checker on Spanish words, determines how to handle Tuteo and Voseo verb forms.
Check spelling as you type	Checks for misspellings as you type words.
Hide spelling and grammar errors	Hides or displays the wavy red lines that appear under misspellings.
Check grammar with spelling	Flags grammatical errors by underlining them in green.

Customize the spelling checker

1 Click File to display the Backstage view.

2 Click Options.

The OneNote Options dialog box opens.

3 Click Proofing.

4 Select the spelling checker options that you want.

5 Click OK.

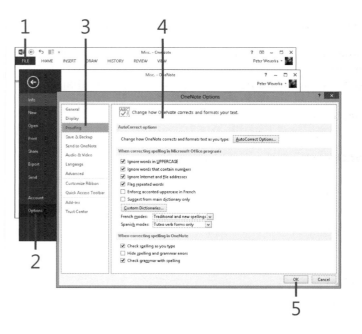

🔍 **SEE ALSO**   To learn how to automatically correct misspellings you commonly make, without having to use the spelling checker, read "Autocorrecting common misspellings" on page 143.

Using the spelling checker with foreign-language text

Besides being able to use the spelling checker with English text, you can use it in other languages. Versions of Office 2013 available in North America come with an English, French, and Spanish dictionary for checking spelling. To use the spelling checker for text in any other language, you can download and install its dictionary from *http://office.microsoft.com/en-us/language/*.

Run a spelling check on foreign-language text

1 Select text written in a foreign language.

You can select a sentence, paragraph, or an entire note.

2 On the ribbon, click the Review tab.

3 Click Language, and then in the drop-down list that appears, choose Set Proofing Language.

The Proofing Language task pane opens.

4 Identify the language in which the text was written.

OneNote checks words you selected in step 1 against the spelling dictionary you selected in this step.

> 🔍 **SEE ALSO** To learn how to correct any errors found in your foreign language text, read "Running the spelling checker" on page 138.

> ➡️ **TRY THIS** When you see several words in a row underlined in red because OneNote thinks that they're misspelled, note whether the words are written in a foreign language. If they are foreign-language words, select the words and identify them as foreign-language text so that OneNote can properly check their spelling.

> 🔍 **SEE ALSO** To learn how to translate text to and from different languages, read "Translating text by using the Mini Translator" on page 201.

Autocorrecting common misspellings

OneNote 2013 (and all the other Office 2013 applications) have a built-in AutoCorrect feature that handles misspellings for you. For example, if you mistype the word "only" by typing "onyl," One-Note corrects the misspelling as soon as you make it. As soon as you type o-n-y-l and press the Spacebar, OneNote corrects the error.

You can use AutoCorrect to do more than automatically correct misspellings. You can also use it to enter hard-to-type jargon, scientific terms, and the like.

Autocorrect common misspellings

1 Click File to display the Backstage view.

2 Click Options.

3 Click Proofing.

4 Click AutoCorrect Options.

5 In the Replace text box, enter a shortcut code or the actual mis-spelling for a hard-to-type term, jargon, or other word.

6 In the With text box, enter the correct spelling for the word or code you entered in step 5.

7 Click Add.

8 Click OK.

From that point forward, if you type the mistake or the shortcut code entered in step 5, OneNote will automatically replace it with the correction entered in step 6.

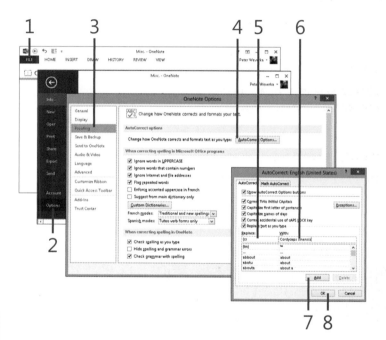

> ⚠️ **CAUTION** If you use AutoCorrect to enter a shortcut code for a hard-to-type term, ensure that you don't enter characters that you might really need in the Replace text box. You could unexpectedly trigger AutoCorrect. For example, if you wanted to type cs and have OneNote replace it with cordyceps sinensis, you might want to type {cs in the Replacement text box instead of just cs. By starting AutoCorrect replacement entries with a curly bracket ({), you make it less likely to trigger AutoCorrect unexpectedly.

Drawing notes

Sometimes saying it with pictures is better than saying it with words, and for those occasions, OneNote offers the Draw tab. This tab presents tools for drawing free-form and preset lines and shapes.

After you make a drawing, you can move it and change its size. You can also erase parts of it. The Draw tab also has tools for rotating drawings and determining how drawings overlap when more than one occupies the same space on a page.

Drawing is easiest if you have a tablet PC or pen device, but you can also draw by dragging the mouse. When you draw, you can choose between lines of various widths, colors, and transparencies.

In this section:

- Drawing free-form with a pen or highlighter
- Creating a free-form pen or highlighter
- Drawing lines, shapes, and graphs
- Using the eraser
- Panning to see your work
- Selecting lines and shapes
- Moving lines and shapes
- Resizing and deleting lines and shapes
- Arranging overlapping lines, shapes, and containers
- Rotating and flipping lines and shapes

Drawing free-form with a pen or highlighter

Drawing free-form with a pen or highlighter presents an opportunity to exercise your creativity. You can draw free-form to illustrate concepts and ideas. To draw free-form, select the pen or highlighter that you want to use and then drag your pen device, finger, or mouse on the page. After you finish drawing, you must inform OneNote 2013 that you want to resume typing notes.

The difference between pens and highlighters is that lines you draw with a highlighter are transparent. You can drag a highlighter across text to call attention to it, for example.

Draw free-form with a pen or highlighter

1 On the ribbon, click the Draw tab.

2 In the Pens gallery, in the Favorite Pens list, select a pen or highlighter.

   This list contains the pens you use most often as well as custom pens or highlighters.

3 Drag with a pen device, mouse, or your finger on the page. To draw using your finger, you must first click Draw With Touch.

4 In the Pens gallery, click the More button to view additional pen and highlighter choices.

(continued on next page)

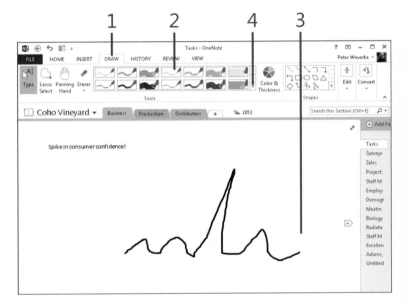

Draw free-form with a pen or highlighter *(continued)*

5 In the Built-In Pens list, select a pen.

6 Drag on the page with this pen.

7 When you finish drawing, press Esc or click Type to resume typing notes.

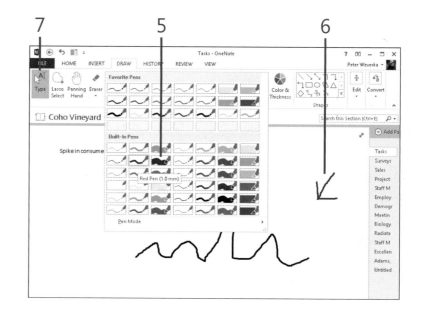

SEE ALSO To learn how to convert a handwritten note to text, read "Handwriting notes and converting them to text" on page 79.

CAUTION You can't draw if OneNote is in Create Handwriting Only mode. To see which mode OneNote is in, open the Pens gallery, select Pen Mode, and then notice which option is selected on the Pen Mode menu. To be able to draw, Create Both Handwriting And Drawings mode or Creating Drawings Only mode must be selected.

Creating a custom pen or highlighter

OneNote 2013 offers options for creating pens and highlighters in the color and width of your choice. After you create a pen or highlighter, it is added to the Favorite Pens list, which appears at the top of the Pens gallery.

To create a custom pen or highlighter, start by designating a pen or highlighter tip, choose a thickness, and then choose a color.

Pens and highlighters that you create are added automatically to the Favorite Pens list. By right-clicking a pen or highlighter in this list, you can move it higher or lower in the list, or remove it altogether.

Create a custom pen or highlighter

1 On the ribbon, click the Draw tab.

2 In the Tools group, click Color & Thickness.

3 In the Color & Thickness dialog box, click the Pen or Highlighter option.

4 Choose a Thickness option.

5 In the line color gallery, choose a Line Color option.

6 Click OK.

The pen or highlighter you created is added to the Favorites Pens list at the top of the Pens gallery.

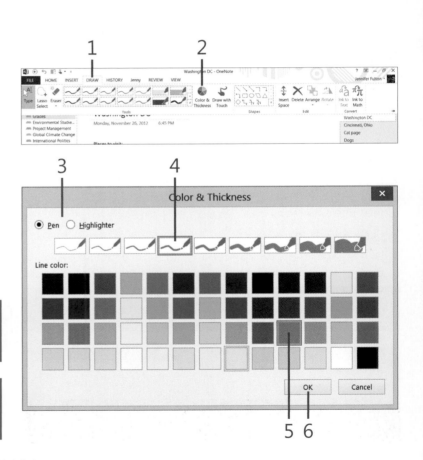

 TIP To remove a pen or highlighter from the Favorite Pens list, right-click the pen or highlighter and then, in the shortcut menu that appears, click Remove Pen From This List.

 TIP You can place a built-in pen or highlighter on the Favorite Pens list in the Pens gallery, where you can access it more easily. Right-click the pen or highlighter and choose Add To Favorite Pens.

Drawing lines, shapes, and graphs

Besides drawing free-form lines with a pen device, mouse, or your finger, you can draw straight lines, shapes, and graphs:

- **Straight lines**   Draw lines, lines with arrows, and lines at 90-degree angles

- **Shapes**   Draw rectangles, ovals, parallelograms, triangles, and diamonds

- **Graphs**   Draw two and three-dimensional graphs

To draw a line, shape, or graph, start by choosing a pen and selecting the preset line, shape, or graph that you want to draw. Then, drag on the page to create the line, shape, or graph in the size you want.

Draw lines, shapes, and graphs

1 On the ribbon, click the Draw tab.

2 In the Tools group, click the More drop-down arrow to open the Pens gallery. (If the pen you want is already visible, you can choose it without clicking the More arrow first.)

3 Choose a pen.

4 In the Insert Shapes gallery, click the More drop-down arrow. (If the shape you want is already visible, you can choose it without clicking the More arrow first.)

5 Choose a line, shape, or graph.

6 On the page, drag with a pen device, mouse, or your finger to draw the line, shape, or graph. (To draw with your finger, you must first click Draw With Touch on the Draw tab.)

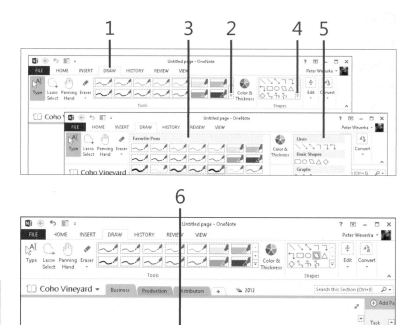

> ✓ **TIP**   To change the thickness and color of a free-form line or shape, select it and then, on the mini-toolbar that appears, click Pen Properties. In the Color & Thickness dialog box that opens, choose a different thickness and line color.

> 🔍 **SEE ALSO**   To learn how to change the size of lines, shapes, and graphs, read "Resizing and deleting lines and shapes" on page 155.

Using the eraser

Use the Eraser to erase all or parts of a free-form line, shape, or graph. OneNote offers two types of erasers:

- **Eraser (small, medium, and large)** Drag over a line with this eraser to remove part of a line.

- **Stroke eraser** Click a line with this eraser to erase an entire stroke (each time you lift the pen device, mouse, or finger, a new stroke is created).

Just as with drawing, you must inform OneNote when you are finished erasing.

Use the eraser

1 On the ribbon, click the Draw tab.

2 In the Tools group, click the Eraser button to open a gallery and choose an eraser.

3 Click to erase a single stroke with the Stroke Eraser, or, using the Small, Medium, or Large Eraser, drag across a line or shape to erase part of it.

4 Press Esc or click Type when you finish erasing to resume typing notes.

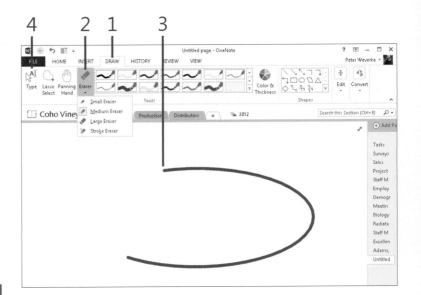

 TIP By erasing parts of lines, you can create new shapes. For example, by erasing part of an oval, you can create an arc.

CAUTION Erasing part of a line or shape breaks the line or shape into separate parts and creates two separate drawings. This is an issue if you want to move the drawing. To move a drawing's various parts, use the Lasso Select tool to select the drawing and then move it.

Panning to see your work

On a OneNote 2013 page that is crowded with many lines and shapes, it can be hard to find the line or shape you are looking for. For this reason, the Draw tab offers the Panning Hand.

With the Panning Hand, you can drag horizontally to move the page from side to side, or drag vertically to move it up or down.

Pan across or down the page

1 On the ribbon, click the Draw tab.

2 In the Tools group, click Panning Hand.

3 On the page, drag the Panning Hand to the left, to the right, up, or down.

4 When you finish panning, press Esc or click Type to resume typing notes.

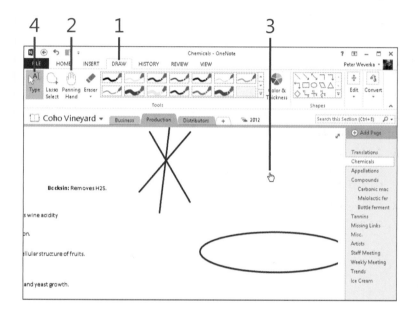

TIP On the Draw tab, click the Insert Space button and drag on the screen to create an empty space for drawing more lines and shapes.

CAUTION You will not see the Panning Hand button if you use a tablet; instead, you can use your as you normally would to pan by dragging up, down, right, or left.

Selecting lines and shapes

Before you can move, resize, or delete a line or shape in One-Note 2013, you have to select it. You can see when you have successfully selected a shape because small white squares called *handles* appear on its sides and corners. You can use these handles to resize a shape. You can also move, delete, and format a selected shape.

To select a line or shape, you can click it, lasso it, or drag over it. Clicking is best to select one line or shape; lassoing or dragging works best for selecting more than one line or shape.

Select a line or shape by clicking

1 On the ribbon, click the Draw tab.

2 In the Tools group, click Type.

3 Move the pointer directly over a line or shape and then click it.

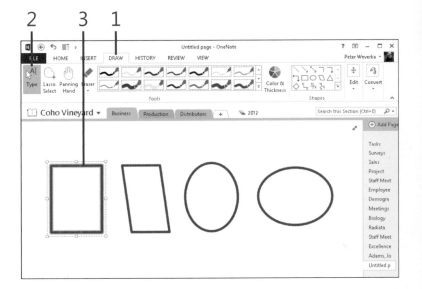

TIP You can also select multiple lines or shapes by dragging over them diagonally.

Select lines and shapes with the Lasso

1 On the ribbon, click the Draw tab.

2 In the Tools group, click Lasso Select.

3 Drag a circle around the lines or shapes that you want to select and then release the mouse button.

4 When you finish selecting the lines or shapes, press Esc or click Type.

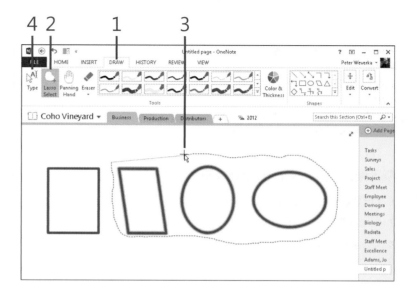

 TIP You can see when lines and shapes are selected because they appear inside a box with dotted lines. In addition, handles appear at the sides and corners of the lines or shapes to show they are selected.

Moving lines and shapes

After you draw lines and shapes, you can move them on the OneNote 2013 page to create illustrations. To move a line or shape, select it and drag. Lines and shapes can be placed over one another (partially obscuring the line or shape underneath) or next to each other to create complex illustrations.

Move lines and shapes

1 On the ribbon, click the Draw tab.

2 In the Tools group, click Type or Lasso Select.

3 Select the line or shape.

4 Move the pointer over the line or shape until you see the four-arrow pointer.

5 Drag the line or shape to a different location.

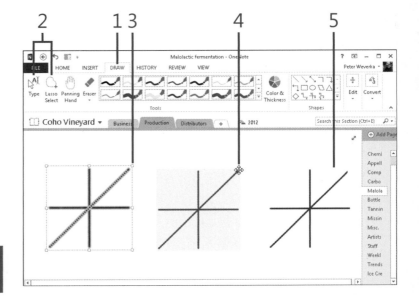

  SEE ALSO To learn techniques for selecting lines and shapes, read "Selecting lines and shapes" on page 152.

TIP You can move several lines and shapes at the same time by selecting them and then dragging.

TIP To help you line up shapes and note containers on pages, OneNote automatically snaps these items to an invisible grid when you move them. If you prefer that items not snap to this grid, on the Insert Shapes gallery, click the More button and clear the Snap To Grid check box. You can also press Alt as you drag items to temporarily turn the grid option off.

Resizing and deleting lines and shapes

As you fashion a OneNote illustration from lines and shapes, you often have to resize the lines and shapes. Sometimes, you have to delete a line or shape, as well.

To change the size of a line or shape, drag one of its handles. By dragging a corner handle, you can retain a shape's proportions as you change its size.

Resize lines and shapes

1 On the ribbon, click the Draw tab.

2 In the Tools group, click Type or Lasso Select.

3 Select a shape.

4 Move the pointer over a handle. When you see the double-arrow pointer, start dragging. Drag inward to make the shape smaller; drag outward to enlarge it.

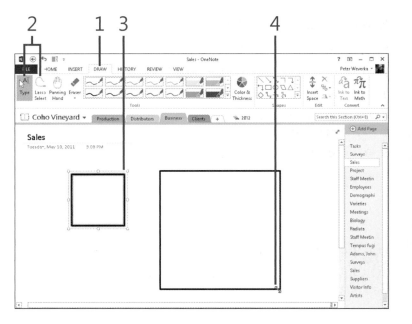

 SEE ALSO To learn techniques for selecting lines and shapes, read "Selecting lines and shapes" on page 152.

TIP To change a shape's size but keep its proportions, drag a corner handle. Drag by a side handle to change the shape's size and proportions at the same time.

Delete lines and shapes

1 On the ribbon, click the Draw tab.

2 In the Tools group, click Type or Lasso Select.

3 Select a line or shape.

4 In the Edit group, click the Delete button (or press Delete).

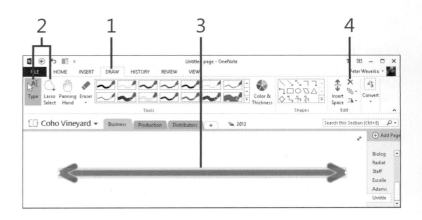

 SEE ALSO To learn how to erase lines and shapes by using the Eraser tool, read "Using the eraser" on page 150.

Arranging overlapping lines, shapes, images, and containers

When lines, shapes, images, and note containers overlap, you can specify which is on top by using an Arrange command on the Draw tab. Objects on a OneNote 2013 page that overlap one another are arranged similar to a stack of plates; their position in the stack determines how much of the object is seen.

For example, if a square and an image overlap, the object on top of the stack is seen fully, and the object at the bottom is covered up, partially or fully, by the object on top.

Start by selecting the line, shape, image, or note container that you want to move up or down in a stack of overlapping items. Then, you can move the object up or down one position in the stack, or all the way to the top or bottom.

Arrange overlapping lines, shapes, images, and containers

1 On the ribbon, click the Draw tab.

2 In the Tools group, click Type or Lasso Select.

3 Select a line, shape, image, or note container in a stack of items.

4 In the Edit group, click Arrange.

5 Choose how to move the object in the stack:

- **Bring Forward**   Raises the item one layer in the stack
- **Bring to Front**   Moves the item to the top of the stack
- **Send Backward**   Lowers the item by one layer in the stack
- **Send to Back**   Moves the item to the bottom of the stack

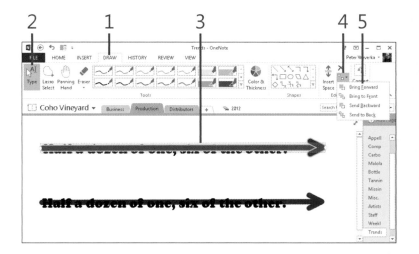

 TIP   Often, you have to repeat the Arrange command until the object is where you want it to be in the stack.

SEE ALSO   To select a note container or image, click it. To learn techniques for selecting lines and shapes, read "Selecting lines and shapes" on page 152.

Rotating and flipping lines and shapes

OneNote 2013 offers commands for flipping items and for rotating items to the left or right by 45 or 90 degrees. Rotating an object pivots it around its center. Flipping an object reverses it (creates a mirror image). An object can be flipped over a horizontal or vertical axis that runs down or across its center.

Rotate and flip lines and shapes

1 On the ribbon, click the Draw tab.

2 In the Tools group, click Type or Lasso Select.

3 Select a line or shape.

4 In the Edit group, click Rotate.

5 On the menu that appears, click any of the Rotate or Flip commands.

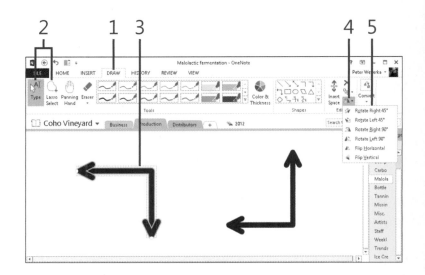

 TIP You can also rotate a line by dragging either handle in a circle.

 TIP You can also apply the Rotate and Flip commands to pictures and screen clippings. However, you can't rotate or flip pictures and screen clippings at 45-degree angles.

Organizing your notes

The more notes you take, the harder it is to stay organized. Notes that should be on one page end up on another. Sometimes pages need to be moved to a different section, and sections need to be moved to a different notebook.

Microsoft OneNote 2013 offers commands for moving and copying pages and sections to different places.

Another way to stay organized and be able to locate notes is to tag them. For example, you can tag notes that require a follow-up with the Important or To Do tag. When you need to find these notes, you can run the Find Tags command. OneNote comes with a selection of readymade tags, and you can create customized tags for your needs.

To help identify notebook and sections, you can color-code them. Devise a color scheme for assigning colors to different topics and then color-code your notebooks, sections, and pages accordingly.

In this section:

- Moving or copying pages
- Moving or copying a section to another notebook
- Tagging notes and other items for follow-up
- Customizing tags
- Deleting tags
- Finding tagged items
- Color-coding notebooks, sections, and pages

Moving or copying pages

No matter how carefully you organize sections, you inevitably have to move and copy pages to a different section. OneNote 2013 offers the following methods for moving and copying pages:

- **Move or copy some pages to a different section**   Move or copy one or more pages from one section to another. Moving the pages deletes them from their original

location; copying the pages retains copies in the original location.

- **Move and copy *all* the pages in a section to a different section (merging)**   Move or copy *all* the pages in a section to a different section.

Move or copy a page or pages

1   In the page tabs, right-click the name of a page.

To move or copy more than one page, select the pages before right-clicking. To select more than one page, Ctrl+click page tabs.

2   On the shortcut menu that appears, click Move Or Copy (or press Ctrl+Alt+M).

3   In the Move Or Copy Pages dialog box, select the section to which you want to move or copy the page.

4   Click either Move or Copy.

The pages are moved or copied to the end of the section you chose in step 3.

> ✓ **TIP**   You can also move and copy pages by dragging. To move a page, drag it from the page tabs to a section name in the section tabs or Notebooks pane. Hold down the Ctrl key as you drag to copy a page to a different section.

> ✓ **TIP**   If you have trouble finding a section in the Move Or Copy Pages dialog box, type its name in the text box. OneNote lists sections with the name you type.

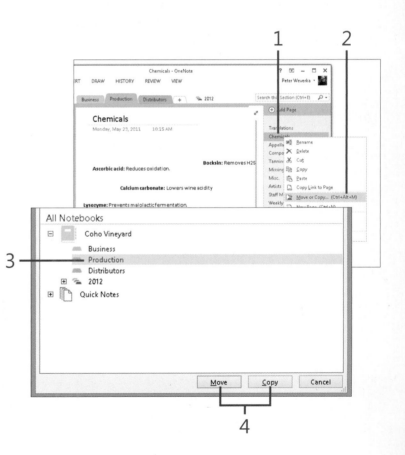

Move or copy all the pages in a section

1   In the Notebooks pane, right-click a section.

2   On the shortcut menu that appears, click Merge Into Another Section.

3   In the Merge Section dialog box, select a section.

4   Click Merge.

5   In the pop-up message box that opens, click Merge Sections.

6   In the next pop-up message box, click Delete to delete the original section and to move, not copy, its pages.

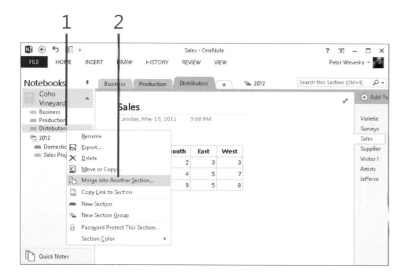

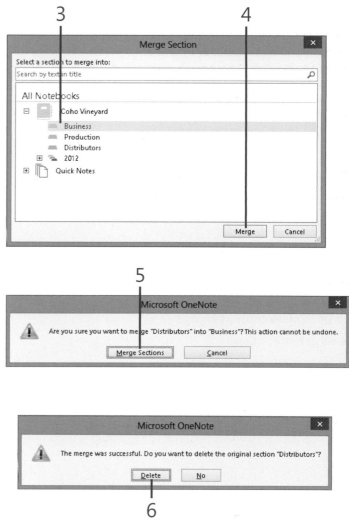

TIP   If you want to retain a copy of a section after you merge its pages with another section, click No in the Merge Was Successful message box.

Moving or copying a section to another notebook

Move or copy a section to another OneNote 2013 notebook if notes you keep will be more useful there. To move or copy a section between notebooks, both notebooks must be open.

Use the Move or Copy command to move or copy a section to another notebook.

Move or copy a section to another notebook

1 In the Notebooks pane, right-click a section.

2 On the shortcut menu that appears, click Move Or Copy.

(continued on next page)

Move or copy a section to another
notebook *(continued)*

3 In the Move Or Copy Section dialog box, select a notebook or a section in the notebook.

4 At the bottom of the dialog box, click either Move or Copy.

3

4

> **TIP** You can also move or copy a section by dragging its name higher or lower in the Notebooks pane. To copy a section, hold down the Ctrl key as you drag the section name.

Tagging notes and other items for follow-up

To make sure that you follow up with notes, consider *tagging* them. Tagging a note means to mark it with an icon.

For example, you can use the To Do tag to mark a note as a task. By using tags, you can quickly identify important notes. Moreover, you can use the Find Tags command to search for notes that you tagged.

OneNote 2013 offers some two dozen tags (To Do, Important, and others) in the Tags gallery on the Home tab. Some of the

tags highlight notes rather than mark notes with icons. Some tags change the font color of notes. You can create your own tags to supplement the tags in the Tags gallery, or customize existing tags.

You can tag a note, paragraph in a note, or page title. You can tag other items, too, such as pictures and audio you've recorded. You can remove a tag when you no longer need it.

Tag a note, other item, or page

1 Click a note (or other item such as a paragraph or table) or page title. Ctrl+click notes or other items if you want to tag several at once (not page titles, however).

2 On the ribbon, click the Home tab.

3 In the Tags group, click the More drop-down arrow on the Tags gallery.

4 In the gallery, select a tag.

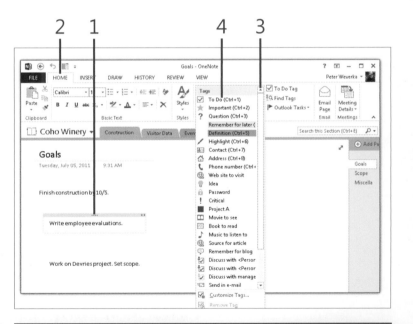

> **TIP** The first nine tags in the Tags gallery are assigned the keyboard shortcuts Ctrl+1 through Ctrl+9. Press one of these keyboard shortcuts to assign a tag listed at the top of the Tags gallery.

> **TIP** You can also tag a note or other item by right-clicking it, pointing to the Tags gallery on the mini-toolbar, and then, in the gallery that opens, selecting a tag.

> **SEE ALSO** To learn how to search for items that you tagged, read "Finding tagged items" on page 169.

Remove a tag from a note, other item, or page

1 Click a tagged note (or other item such as a paragraph or picture) or a page title. Ctrl+click items to remove the tags from several notes or other items at once (not page titles, however).

2 On the ribbon, click the Home tab.

3 In the Tags group, click the More drop-down arrow on the Tags gallery.

4 In the gallery, select Remove Tag.

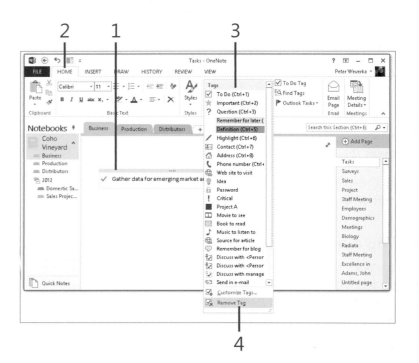

Customizing tags

OneNote 2013 offers more than two dozen tags in the Tags gallery, but if they aren't descriptive enough to suit your needs, you can create tags of your own or modify existing tags.

When you create a tag, OneNote gives you the opportunity to choose a descriptive name for it, a symbol, and a font color or highlight color to make your tag easy to identify.

Customize a tag

1 On the ribbon, click the Home tab.

2 In the Tags group, click the More drop-down arrow on the Tags gallery.

3 In the gallery, select Customize Tags.

(continued on next page)

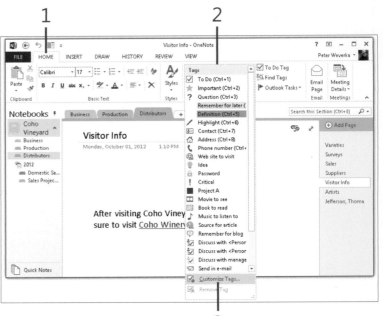

Customize a tag *(continued)*

4 In the Customize Tags dialog box, click New Tag.

5 In the New Tag dialog box, in the Display name text box, enter a name.

6 Choose a symbol.

Watch the preview area as you construct your tag—it shows what your tag will look like when you finish creating it.

7 If you want, choose a font color or highlight color.

8 Click OK (and click OK again in the Custom Tags dialog box).

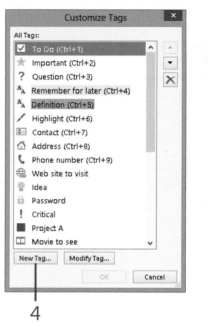

✓ **TIP** The first nine tags in the Tags gallery are assigned the shortcut keys Ctrl+1 through Ctrl+9. To assign a keyboard shortcut to a customized tag, move the customized tag to one of the first nine positions in the Tags gallery. To move a tag, in the Customize Tags dialog box, select it and click the Move Tag Up or Move Tag Down button.

→ **TRY THIS** Rather than customize a tag, choose one of the numerous tags in the Tags gallery and modify it. In the Tags gallery, right-click a tag and then, in the shortcut menu that appears, choose Modify This Tag. The Modify Tag dialog box opens, in which you can modify the tag.

Deleting tags

The Tags gallery in OneNote 2013 offers many tags. To make locating the tags you use easier, consider deleting the tags you don't use. Tags you delete from the Tags gallery remain on notes and other items that you tagged previously. For example, if you tag notes with the Book To Read tag but subsequently delete that tag from the gallery, the Book To Read tag remains on the notes to which you originally applied it.

Delete a tag

1 On the ribbon, click the Home tab.

2 In the Tags group, click the More drop-down arrow on the Tags gallery.

3 Right-click the tag that you want to delete.

4 On the shortcut menu that appears, choose Delete This Tag.

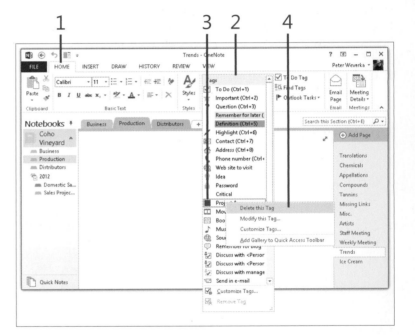

TIP You can also delete a tag in the Customize Tags dialog box. Open the Tags gallery and choose Customize Tags to open this dialog box. Select the tag that you want to delete and click Remove.

Finding tagged items

OneNote 2013 provides the Tags Summary pane for locating tagged notes and other items such as page titles and tables. After you conduct a search for tagged items, you can click an item in the search results and go directly to the tag.

When you open the Tags Summary pane, it lists all tagged items. Use this pane to narrow the scope of the search and instruct OneNote how to arrange, or group, items found in the search.

- **Group Tags By** Arrange search results in the Tags Summary pane by tag name (Tag Name), section name

(Section), page title (Title), date (Date), or alphabetical order by note content (Note Text).

- **Show Only Unchecked Items** Search for tags with a check box symbol (the To Do tag, for example) to locate only items that have not been checked off.

- **Search** Limit the scope for the search to the current page group, section group, section, or notebook. You can also limit the scope to a particular time period.

Find tagged items

1 On the ribbon, click the Home tab.

2 In the Tags group, click Find Tags.

3 Choose how to group the search results.

4 Choose a search scope such as this section (Section) or this week's notes (Date).

5 Click an item to go to the tag.

> ✓ **TIP** Click the Refresh Results button in the Tags Summary pane when you want to update the results of the search. Update the search if you make changes to tagged items and want to get an up-to-date accounting of where the tags are.

> → **TRY THIS** In the Tags Summary pane, click Create Summary Page to create a new page with a copy of all tagged items found in your search. Copying the items to a new page is a convenient way to have a look at all tagged items you found.

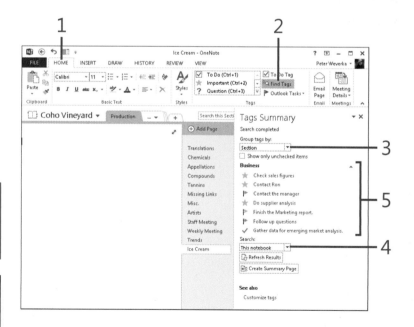

Color-coding notebooks, sections, and pages

You can color-code OneNote 2013 notebooks, sections, and pages to make it easier to recognize and find notes. For example, to distinguish notes pertaining to a specific project, make pages where those notes are kept green. However, when you color a page, its background is changed, but not the color of its page tab.

To quickly identify a section by color, color-code its tab with a specific color. Color-code notebooks to help distinguish one notebook from another in the Notebooks pane. When you color a notebook, its icon in the Notebooks pane is changed to that color.

Color-code a page

1 On the ribbon, click the View tab.

2 In the page tabs, select a page.

3 In the Page Setup group, click Page Color.

4 In the gallery that opens, choose a color.

The background of the page is changed to the color you selected.

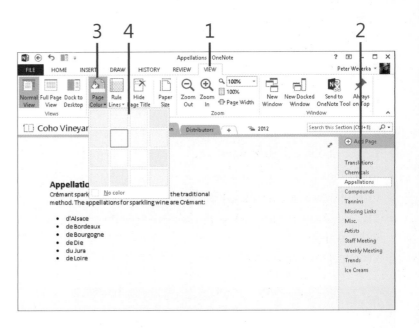

Color-code a section

1 Right-click a section tab.

2 On the shortcut menu that appears, point to Section Color.

3 In the submenu, click a color.

The section tab is changed to the color you selected.

Searching for stray notes

In this section:

- Searching for a note on a page
- Searching a section, section group, or notebook
- Searching for notes in all open notebooks
- Refining searches with the Search Results pane
- Choosing the default search scope

Microsoft OneNote 2013 provides the Search box for finding stray notes. This box is located in the upper right of the screen, above the page tabs. To conduct a search, enter a search term in the Search box.

You can restrict searches to the currently open page, section, section group, notebook, or all open notebooks. You can also choose what OneNote searches by default.

When you search the currently open page, the term you entered is highlighted on the page so you can find notes that contain that term. When searching sections, section groups, and notebooks, pages where the search term is found are listed. By clicking a page name in the results list, you can preview the page where the search term was found; the search term is highlighted on the page so that you can find it easily.

After your initial search you can open the Search Results pane, change the scope of your search, and sort the search results by section name, page title, or date modified.

Searching for a note on a page

To locate a note on the currently open page, you need to specify that to OneNote 2013.

After you enter a search term, instances of the term are highlighted in yellow on the page, and OneNote lists how many matches it found. You can clearly see notes with the search term you entered. Scroll the page or click the Next Match (or Previous Match) button to find the note for which you're searching.

Search a page

1 Open the page that you want to search.

2 Click the Change Search Scope down-arrow.

3 In the drop-down list that opens, click Find On This Page.

4 Type a search term in the Search box.

Matches are highlighted in yellow on the page, and the page scrolls to display the first match.

5 Click the Next Match button (or press F3) to view the next match.

6 Click the Previous Match button (or press Shift+F3) to return to the previous match.

7 To end the search, in the Search box, click the Close button (or press Esc).

TIP Search terms are not case-sensitive. You can enter search terms without regard to how they are capitalized in your notes.

TIP The fastest way to conduct a page search is to press Ctrl+F. Pressing Ctrl+F chooses Find On This Page as the search scope and places the cursor in the Search box.

SEE ALSO To learn how to change the scope of a search and sort the search results differently, read "Refining searches with the Search Results pane" on page 177.

CAUTION The Search box does not appear in Full Page view. Press Ctrl+E or switch to Normal view to display the Search box when you are in Full Page view.

Searching a section, section group, or notebook

To search a section, section group, or notebook, start by opening a page in the section, section group, or notebook in which you want to search. Then, enter a search term and limit the search scope to This Section, This Section Group, or This Notebook. OneNote 2013 conducts the search and lists pages with notes containing your search term, even if those pages are in the Recycle Bin. OneNote also lists pages that contain the term only in the page title.

In the On Page section of the search results list, you'll find pages that contain the search term that you have not yet visited. As you preview pages, they appear in the Recent Picks section, instead.

By clicking a page name in the search results, you can preview the page, and the search results list remains open so that you can continue to preview each result. When you click a page that you are previewing, OneNote closes the search results list.

Search a section, section group, or notebook

1 Open the section, section group, or notebook that you want to search.

2 Click or tap the Change Search Scope down-arrow.

3 In the drop-down list that opens, click or tap This Section, This Section Group, or This Notebook.

4 Type a term in the Search box.

5 Click or tap a page name in the search results to preview the page. Continue to select page names to preview pages and locate the page you want.

6 To close the search results list, in the Search box, click the Close button, press Esc, or click the page you're previewing.

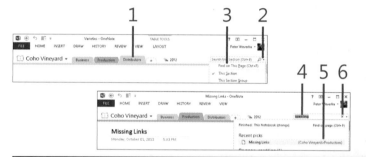

 CAUTION The Search box does not appear in Full Page view. Press Ctrl+E or switch to Normal view to display the Search box when you are in Full Page view.

 TIP Search terms are not case-sensitive. You can enter any combination of uppercase and lowercase letters as a search term.

→ **TRY THIS** Search for a phrase by enclosing the phrase in quotation marks. Type "**york** and "**new**" on one page, and "**New York**" on another. Then, type "**new york**" in the Search box, and note that both pages appear in the results, because both pages contain both of the words you searched for. Type "**new york**" as the search term, and notice that only the page with both words in that order appears.

✓ **TIP** Click the Pin Search Results link to display results in the Search Results pane. The pane remains open even after you click a page and make edits.

🔍 **SEE ALSO** To learn how to change the scope of a search and sort the search results differently, read "Refining searches with the Search Results pane" on page 177.

Searching for notes in all open notebooks

To search more than one notebook, the notebooks must be open. Ensure that the Notebook pane lists all notebooks that you want to search before you start searching more than one notebook.

In a search of all notebooks, all pages on which the search term is found are listed. Pages with the search term in the Recycle Bin and pages with the search term only in the title are listed, as well. For each page, OneNote lists the notebook and section in which the page is located. This helps you to quickly identify the page you're trying to find.

Click a page name to preview a page. Notes on the page with your search term are highlighted in yellow. Click a page to edit the page and dismiss the search results list.

Search all open notebooks

1 Open the notebooks that you want to search (ensure that their names appear in the Notebook pane).

2 Click the Change Search Scope down-arrow.

3 Click All Notebooks.

4 Type a term in the Search box.

5 Click a page in the search results list to preview a page with the search term. Continue to click page names to preview pages and locate the page you want.

6 To close the search results list, in the Search box, click the Close button, press Esc, or click the page you're previewing.

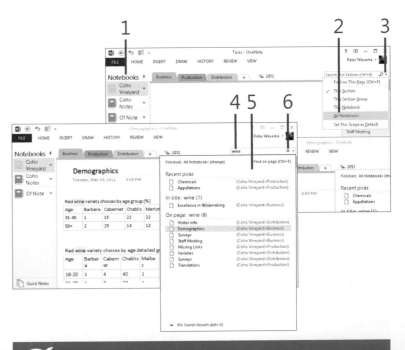

> **! CAUTION** OneNote can search only notebooks that are open. If you can't find a note, it could be because it is located in a notebook that is closed or a section that is password-protected and currently locked. Open the notebook or unlock the section and try the search again.

> **SEE ALSO** To learn how to change the scope of a search and sort the search results differently, read "Refining searches with the Search Results pane" on page 177.

> **✓ TIP** Click the Pin Search Results link to display results in the Search Results pane. The pane remains open, even after you click or tap a page and make edits.

Refining searches with the Search Results pane

Sometimes after conducting a search, you need to expand or narrow the search parameters to make it easier to find the note for which you're searching. For example, if you searched for notes in all notebooks and ended up with a long list of results, you might want to limit the search to the current notebook or section only.

To refine searches, you should pin open the Search Results pane so that you can easily change the search parameters and the order in which results appear. The Search Results pane offers two methods of refining a search:

- The Change Search Scope menu presents options to expand or narrow the notebooks, sections, and section

groups included in your search. Expand a search, for example, when the initial search fails to produce any results; narrow a search when the search produces too many results.

- The Sort By menu presents options for sorting the search results. You can sort the results by section, page title, or date modified.

Click a page name in the Search Results pane to preview the page. The Search Results pane not only lists the names of pages, it also shows note contents. Seeing the contents of notes helps you to identify the note for which you're looking.

Refine a search

1 Type a term in the Search box.

2 Click the Change Search Scope down-arrow and choose the area you want to search, such as This Section.

3 Click Pin Search Results (or press Alt+O) to open the Search Results pane so that you can change the search parameters.

(continued on next page)

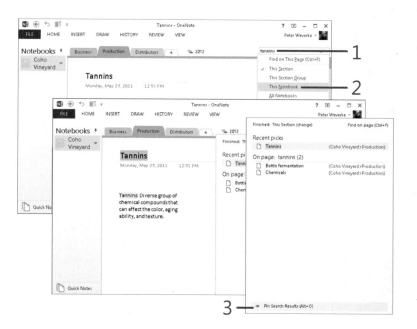

Refine a search *(continued)*

4 Open the Change Scope menu and choose a different scope for the search if desired. For example, choose This Notebook.

5 Open the Sort By menu and choose a different sort order for the results list if desired. For example, choose Sort By Date Modified.

6 Click a page in the search results list to preview a page. Continue to click page names to preview pages and locate the page you want.

7 To close the search results list, in the Search box, click the Close button, press Esc, or click the page you're previewing.

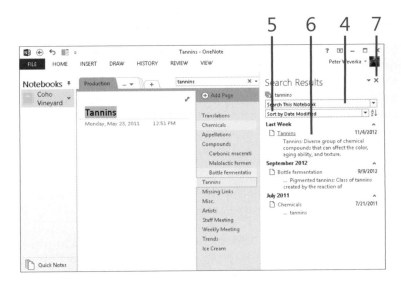

✓ **TIP** In addition to sorting the search results by section, page title, or date modified, you can designate whether the results appear in ascending or descending order. An ascending sort arranges search results from A to Z or from the earliest in time to the latest in time. A descending sort arranges search results from Z to A or from the latest in time to the earliest in time. For example, if you choose to sort the results list by page title in descending order, results appear with page names arranged in reverse alphabetical order. If you choose to sort by date modified and ascending order, results appear with the pages modified most recently at the top of the list. Click the Sort Ascending or Sort Descending button in the Search Results pane to change the sort order.

Choosing the default search scope

When you conduct a search, OneNote 2013 initially searches by using the default scope selection: This Section, This Section Group, This Notebook, or All Notebooks. You can change the default search scope so that initial searches find notes in the area of your choice, but you cannot set the default to search the current page only.

You can, however, override the default search scope prior to searching. For example, if you normally want to search the current notebook, set the default search scope to This Notebook. That way, whenever you search, OneNote automatically searches the current notebook. If you want to search all notebooks (to widen the search), or the current page only (to narrow the results), you can choose a different search area prior to searching.

Set the default search scope

1 Click the Change Search Scope down-arrow.

2 Choose the option that you want as the default search scope.

3 Open the Change Search Scope menu again and choose Set This Scope As Default.

> ✓ **TIP** You can always change the search scope in the middle of a search by opening the Change Search Scope menu and choosing an option.

> ✓ **TIP** If you're not sure what the default scope selection is, just glance at the Search box. If, for example, it reads "Search This Section," OneNote is set to search the current section by default. If it reads "Search," All Notebooks is the default scope, and unless you choose a different search scope, all notebooks are searched.

> → **TRY THIS** Set the default search scope to All Notebooks. Then, search for a word you commonly use in your notes to see how many results you get. Change the default scope to something narrower, such as This Section, and then search again. After trying this experiment, decide what you want your search scope to be by default and then set it.

Housecleaning in OneNote

Sometimes it's necessary to delete a page or section when you no longer need it. Deleting unwanted sections and pages keeps your notebook from getting crowded. However, pages and sections that you delete are not really deleted; they are placed in a Recycle Bin. Microsoft OneNote 2013 maintains one Recycle Bin for each notebook you create. Sections and pages remain in the Recycle Bin for 60 days or until you empty the Recycle Bin yourself. To recover a page or section, you can open the Recycle Bin and get it from there.

Notebooks are backed up automatically. You can decide where to keep backup copies of notebooks, how often to back them up, and how many backup copies to keep on hand. Moreover, you can manually back up a notebook whenever you want. OneNote provides the Open Backups command for examining and copying notes, pages, and sections in backup copies of notebooks.

In this section:

- Deleting pages
- Deleting a section
- Restoring pages and sections from the Recycle Bin
- Backing up notebooks on your own
- Choosing how to back up notebooks
- Opening a backup copy of a notebook section

Deleting pages

When you no longer need a page in OneNote 2013, delete it. You can delete more than one page at a time. Deleted pages are placed in the Recycle Bin. If you regret deleting a page, you can recover it from the Recycle Bin.

Delete a page

1 On the page tabs along the right side of the window, click the name of the page that you want to delete.

2 Right-click or the page name, and in the shortcut menu that appears, click Delete.

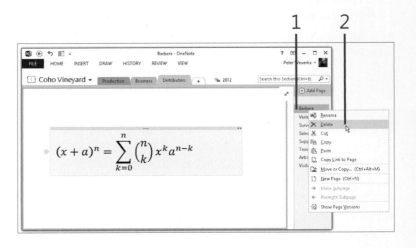

Delete multiple pages

1 On the ribbon, click the Home tab.

2 Ctrl+click page names on the page tabs to select more than one. To select adjoining pages, click the first and Shift+click the last (click the first page, hold down the Shift key, and click the last page).

3 In the Basic Text group, click the Delete button.

TIP Click Undo to restore pages that you just deleted.

SEE ALSO To learn how to recover a page that you deleted, read "Restoring pages and sections from the Recycle Bin" on page 185.

SEE ALSO To learn how to display and collapse the page tabs, read "Collapsing and expanding the Notebooks pane and page tabs" on page 128.

Deleting a section

Delete a section when you no longer need it. When you delete a section, all the pages in that section are deleted as well. Sections you delete are placed in the Recycle Bin in case you want to resuscitate them.

You can delete only one section at a time. When you delete a section, its tab is removed from the top of the OneNote 2013 window. Be careful when deleting sections. The only way to restore a deleted section is to fish it from the Recycle Bin. You can't click Undo to restore a section you deleted.

Delete a section

1 In the Notebooks pane, right-click the name of a section.

2 In the shortcut menu that appears, click Delete.

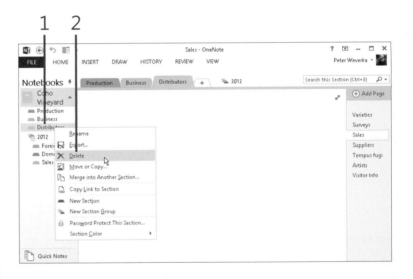

 CAUTION You can't restore a section you deleted by clicking Undo.

 SEE ALSO To learn how to recover a section you deleted, read "Restoring pages and sections from the Recycle Bin" on page 185.

TIP You can also delete a section by right-clicking its tab. In the shortcut menu that appears, click Delete.

Restoring pages and sections from the Recycle Bin

Pages and sections that you delete in OneNote 2013 go to the Recycle Bin, where they remain for 60 days or until you delete them on your own. As long as 60 days have not passed since you deleted a page or section, you can restore it.

In the Recycle Bin, deleted pages are stored on the Deleted Pages tab. The names of deleted sections appear as section tabs. To restore a page or section from the Recycle Bin, move the page or section back to your notebook by using the Move or Copy command.

Restore a page from the Recycle Bin

1 On the ribbon, click the History tab.

2 Click the Notebook Recycle Bin button

The Recycle Bin appears.

3 Click the Deleted Pages tab.

4 Right-click a page name on the page tabs and click Move Or Copy (or press Ctrl+Alt+M).

The Move Or Copy Pages dialog box opens.

(continued on next page)

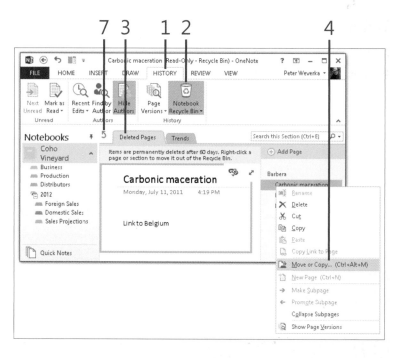

Restore a page from the Recycle Bin *(continued)*

5 Click the section to which you want to restore the page.

6 Click the Move button.

7 Click the Navigate To Parent Section Group button to return to your notebook. (Refer to the screenshot on the previous page.)

5

Move or Copy Pages	✕

Move or copy page to:

Search by text in title   🔍

Recent picks
　　Unfiled Notes　　　　　　　　　　(Quick Notes)

All Notebooks
　⊟　　Coho Vineyard
　　　　　Business
　　　　　Production
　　　　　Distributors
　　⊞　2012
　⊞　　Quick Notes

Move　　Copy　　Cancel

6

 TIP   The fastest way to restore a page from the Recycle Bin is to drag it to the Notebooks pane.

 TIP   You can restore more than one page by Ctrl+clicking to select more than one page on the page tabs.

 SEE ALSO   To learn the details of moving (and copying) pages, read "Moving or copying pages" on page 160.

Restore a section from the Recycle Bin

1 On the ribbon, click the History tab.

2 Click the Notebook Recycle Bin button to open the Recycle Bin.

The Recycle Bin opens.

3 Right-click a section name on the section tabs and click Move Or Copy.

The Move Or Copy Pages dialog box opens.

4 Click a notebook or section to indicate where you want to restore the section.

5 Click the Move button.

6 Click the Navigate To Parent Section Group button to return to your notebook.

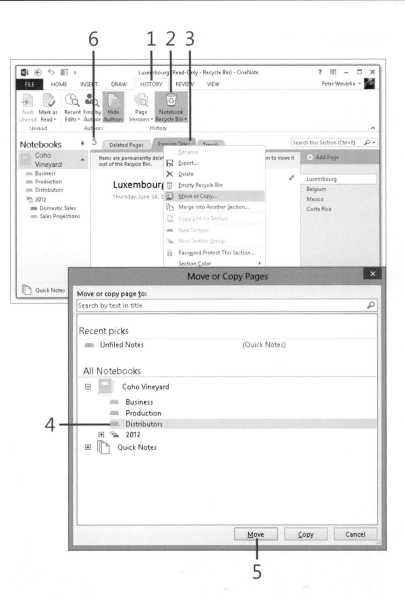

> **TIP** To empty the Recycle Bin, click the History tab, open the menu on the Notebook Recycle Bin button, and then click Empty Recycle Bin. Empty the Recycle Bin occasionally to keep it from getting too cluttered.

> **SEE ALSO** To learn the details of moving (and copying) sections, read "Moving or copying a section to another notebook" on page 162.

Backing up notebooks on your own

In computer lingo, *backing up* means to make a copy of a file on your computer. Back up OneNote notebooks as insurance against a computer failure or other loss of data. If something wicked this way comes and you lose your data, you can recover it from the backup copy.

OneNote backs up all notebooks automatically. However, you can back up a notebook at any time on your own. When you give the command to back up notebooks, you are offered the choice to back up all of your notebooks or back up only the notebooks that have changed since the last time you backed up your OneNote data.

Back up notebooks on your own

1 On the ribbon, click the File tab to display the Backstage view.

2 Click the Options tab.

The OneNote Options dialog box opens.

3 Click Save & Backup.

4 Click Back Up All Notebooks Now.

A message box tells you that the backup is complete.

5 Click OK to close the message box.

6 Click OK to close the dialog box.

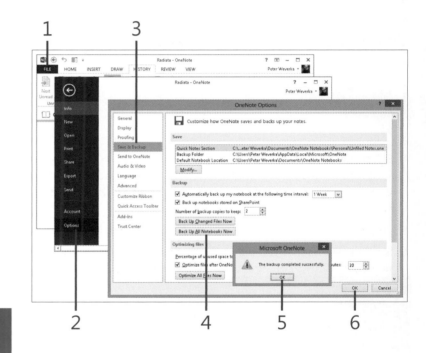

TIP Click Back Up Changed Files Now to back up only notebooks that have been edited since they were last backed up.

 SEE ALSO To learn how to set the interval for automatic backups of OneNote notebooks, see "Choosing how to back up notebooks" on page 189.

Choosing how to back up notebooks

OneNote makes backup copies of all your notebooks automatically. How the backups are made is up to you. You can choose how often notebooks are backed up and how many backup copies to keep.

If your computer is making strange noises and seems always on the verge of failure, back up early and often. Otherwise, back up your OneNote data as often as you think is necessary to keep the data safe and secure.

You can keep multiple backups; when you make a new backup, it replaces the oldest backup copy.

Choose how to back up notebooks

1 On the ribbon, click the File tab to display the Backstage view.

2 Click the Options tab.

The OneNote Options dialog box opens.

3 Click Save & Backup.

4 Select the Automatically Back Up My Notebook At The Following Time Interval check box. To back up any notebooks you've saved on SharePoint, select the Back Up Notebooks Stored On SharePoint check box.

5 Specify how often you want OneNote to back up your notebooks.

6 From the Number Of Backup Copies to Keep menu, specify the number of backup copies you want OneNote to keep.

7 Click OK.

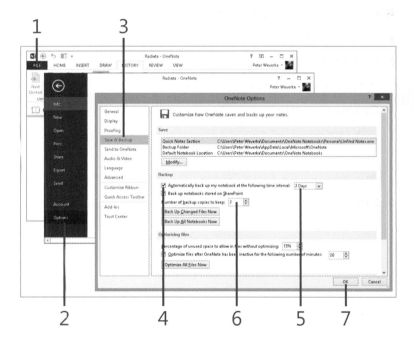

✓ **TIP** If you prefer not to keep backup copies of a notebook, click the History tab, click Notebook Recycle Bin, and on the menu that appears, click Disable History For This Notebook.

Opening a backup copy of a notebook section

OneNote keeps backup copies of your notebooks. These backup copies of notebooks are maintained in the form of sections. The sections have the file extension .one. For example, the backup copy of a section called "Production" is called "Production.one." To help identify when backup copies were made, OneNote lists the date they were made after the backup name.

After you open a backup copy of a section, OneNote places a tab on the Notebooks pane called Open Sections. With this tab, you can switch back and forth between backup sections you opened and your OneNote notebook. You can also copy notes, pages, and the section itself from the backup copy into a notebook.

Open a backup copy of a notebook section

1 On the ribbon, click the File tab to display the Backstage view.

2 Click the Info tab.

3 Click Open Backups.

The Open Backup dialog box opens.

(continued on next page)

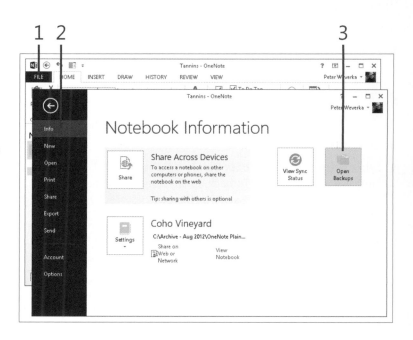

Open a backup copy of a notebook
section *(continued)*

4 Locate the backup copy of the section that you want to open, click it to select it, and then click Open.

The section opens and displays in the OneNote window.

5 When you finish examining the backup section, click a section in the Notebooks pane to return to your notebook.

(continued on next page)

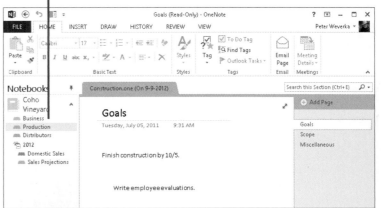

Open a backup copy of a notebook section *(continued)*

6   In the Notebook pane, click Open Sections to switch to the backup section.

7   Click the name of the backup notebook section to return to it.

8   On the section tabs, right-click the backup section's tab and on the shortcut menu that appears, click Close to exit the backup section.

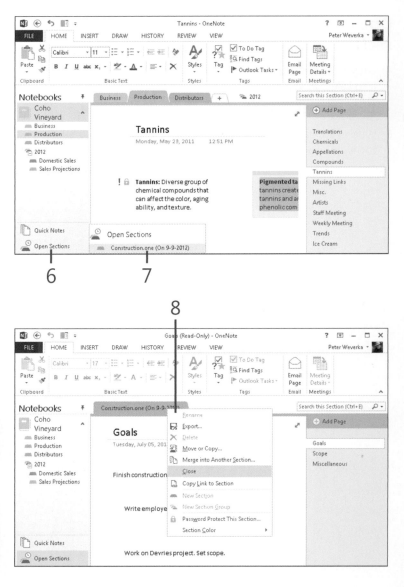

6   **7**

8

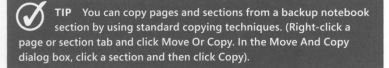

TIP   You can copy pages and sections from a backup notebook section by using standard copying techniques. (Right-click a page or section tab and click Move Or Copy. In the Move And Copy dialog box, click a section and then click Copy).

TRY THIS   To find out where the Backup folder is located, click the File tab, click Options, and click Save & Backup. Then, in the Save section, look for the path to the Backup folder. You can double-click this path in the OneNote Options dialog box to open the Backup folder in the Select Folder dialog box.

Conducting research in OneNote 2013

14

Microsoft OneNote 2013 offers task panes to simplify certain tasks, such as checking the spelling of your notes, identifying foreign language text, looking up a synonym in the Thesaurus, and conducting research via the Internet.

The Research task pane is particularly helpful because it offers dictionaries, a thesaurus, Internet searching, and translation services. And best of all, you can conduct your research inside OneNote without having to open a web browser separately, because the Research task pane works hand in hand with OneNote to make your researching easier.

The Research task pane is available in all Microsoft Office 2013 applications as well as OneNote. You can take advantage of this nifty tool wherever you go in Office.

In this section:

- Understanding task panes
- Researching a topic by using the Internet
- Customizing the Research task pane
- Translating a foreign word or phrase
- Translating text by using the Mini Translator
- Finding the right word by using the Thesaurus

Understanding task panes

OneNote provides task panes to help you perform many different kinds of tasks, from checking the spelling of your notes to conducting research. Task panes provide convenient access to the options related to a particular task, but they do have one drawback: they can get in the way. You can, however, open and close task panes very easily. You can also move, resize, and dock them along the edge of the screen with a few simple techniques.

To open a task pane, on the ribbon, click the Review tab and then click the associated button. For example, when you click the Spelling button, the Spelling task pane appears on the right. Close it by clicking the task pane's Close button (the "X" in the upper-right corner). You can also close a task pane by clicking its button on the Review tab. For example, to close the Spelling task pane, click the Spelling button again.

If you want to continue to use a task pane but it's in the way, you can move it to a different part of the screen, away from its docked position on the right side of the window. When you want, you can easily re-dock the task pane. To move a task pane, hover the mouse pointer over the task pane's title bar. Drag the task pane by its title bar to move it into the middle of the screen. To re-dock the task pane, double-click its title bar or drag it to the right side of the screen until it docks automatically.

Drag to resize   Close button

TIP   You can move a task pane by opening the Task Pane Options menu (by clicking the down arrow at the right end of the task pane's title bar), and choosing Move. In addition, you can resize a task pane by choosing Size from the Options menu.

You can reduce the amount of space a task pane occupies on the right side of the screen while it's docked by resizing it. You can also make a docked task pane wider, if needed. To do so, hover the pointer over the left boundary of the docked task pane, then drag the boundary to the left or right.

If a task pane has been moved into the center of the screen, you can resize it by hovering the pointer over its lower-right corner and dragging the corner.

Drag to move

SEE ALSO To learn how to look up synonyms with the Thesaurus task pane, read "Finding the right word by using the Thesaurus" on page 203.

SEE ALSO To learn how to translate foreign text, read "Translating a foreign word or phrase" on page 200.

SEE ALSO To check the spelling of your notes with the Spelling task pane, read "Running the spelling checker" on page 138 to learn how.

SEE ALSO To learn how to perform research using the Research task pane, read "Researching a topic by using the Internet" on page 196.

Researching a topic by using the Internet

Use the Research task pane when you need more information for a note. The Research task pane offers dictionaries, thesauruses, and Internet searching.

For researching online, the Research task pane offers three choices: Bing, Factiva iWorks, and Highbeam Research. When you conduct an Internet search, you can click a hyperlink in the Research task pane to open a website in your browser.

Speaking of web browsers, the Research task pane, like a browser, offers Back and Forward buttons so that you can retrace or revisit search results.

Research a topic by using the Internet

1 On the ribbon, click the Review tab.

2 Click Research.

The Research task pane opens on the right side of the screen.

3 In the Search For text box, enter a term or terms that describe the topic about which you want information.

4 Open the Services list down-arrow, and in the drop-down list that appears, click a research site such as Bing (or All Research Sites).

5 Scroll through the Research task pane to examine the results of your search.

(continued on next page)

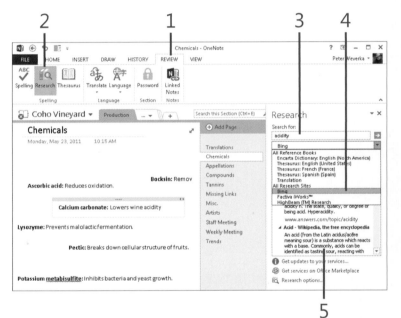

TIP You can use the Research task pane to look up a word's definition. With a word selected, click Encarta Dictionary from the Services list.

Research a topic by using the
Internet *(continued)*

6 Click a link at the bottom of a search result to display it in your browser.

7 Click the Close button to close the Research task pane.

TIP Rather than enter a search term, you can right-click a word or selected phrase, and on the shortcut menu that appears, click Look Up to quickly open the Research task pane and conduct a search.

SEE ALSO To learn how to select which options appear in the Services list, read "Customizing the Research task pane" on page 198.

Customizing the Research task pane

To conduct a search in the Research task pane, you open the Services list and choose a reference book or research site. Which options appear in this list is up to you. OneNote 2013 offers many different options for the Services list.

For faster and better researching, confine the options on the Services list to options you like the best or use the most. You can also designate one choice as your favorite. The Favorite option is the one that is used when you right-click a word in a note and click Look Up.

Customize the Research task pane

1 On the ribbon, click the Review tab.

2 Click Research.

   The Research task pane opens on the right side of the screen.

3 Click Research Options.

   The Research Options dialog box opens.

4 Click the services that you want to appear in the Services list in the Research task pane.

5 Click OK.

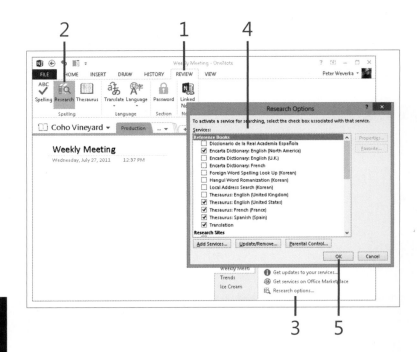

> **→ TRY THIS** Click a service in the Research Options dialog box and click the Properties button. A dialog box appears and describes in detail what the option is.

> **✓ TIP** On the Research task pane, click the Get Services On Office Marketplace link to view a list of additional services that you might want to install, such as FindLaw, Ovid, and Thomson Company Profiles.

Select a favorite research tool

1 On the ribbon, click the Review tab.

2 Click Research.

The Research task pane opens on the right side of the screen.

3 Click Research Options.

The Research Options dialog box opens.

4 Click the option that you want to use by default when you conduct research (this option is used when you right-click a word in a note and click Look Up).

5 Click Favorite.

6 Click OK.

Translating a foreign word or phrase

OneNote 2013 offers the opportunity to translate text not just from English to a foreign language but also from one foreign language to another. After the translation is complete, you can copy it to the Clipboard and paste it in a note.

Translate a word or phrase

1 Drag to select the word or phrase that you want to translate (if you want to translate a single word, simply click that word).

2 On the ribbon, click the Review tab.

3 Click Translate.

4 Click Translate Selected Text.

5 In the From drop-down list, click the language in which the text you selected is written.

6 In the To drop-down list, click the language to which you want to translate the text.

7 Click the Start Searching button.

A translation appears in the Microsoft Translator section of the task pane.

8 Click Insert and choose Insert to insert the translation on the page.

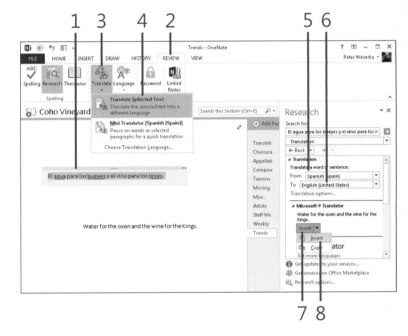

TIP A fast way to translate text is to select it, right-click it, and click Translate on the shortcut menu. OneNote translates the text using the previous From and To options you selected. Choose different From and To options if necessary and then click the Start Searching button to complete the translation.

TIP You can replace the foreign text with the translation by clicking Insert in step 8 and clicking Insert again.

TRY THIS Click the Translation Options link in the Research task pane to open the Translation Options dialog box. It shows all the available language pairs (the To and From translation options). If the To and From language pair you need isn't in the Research task pane, click it in this dialog box so you can translate text to and from the languages of your choice.

Translating text by using the Mini Translator

Another way to translate text is to take advantage of a little device called the Mini Translator. To use it, all you need to do is select the text, hover the pointer over the text, and read the translation in the Microsoft Translator toolbar. But before you can use the Mini Translator, you need to do some setup work.

With the Mini Translator, you can translate text from English to a foreign language, such as French or Spanish. You can also translate text from one foreign language to another or from a foreign language to English.

Translating text with the Mini Translator is a two-part process. First you select the language to which you want to translate the text. Then you use the Mini Translator to produce a translation.

Select a language for the Mini Translator

1 On the ribbon, click the Review tab.

2 Click Translate.

3 Click Choose Translation Language.

The Translation Language Options dialog box opens.

4 In the Translate To drop-down list, choose the language to which you will translate text when using the Mini Translator.

5 Click OK.

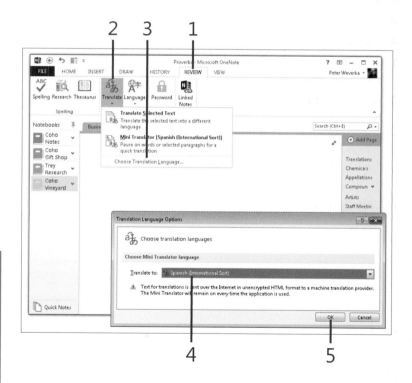

> ⚠️ **CAUTION**   The Mini Translator assumes that your text is written in English (the default proofing language) and that you want to translate text from English to the language you select in step 4. If the text is in a foreign language and you want to translate it into English, you need to identify the text first by selecting it, clicking Review, clicking Language, and then clicking Set Proofing Language. In the Proofing task pane, choose the language in which the text was written and then follow these two tasks to translate it into English or another language by using the Mini Translator.

Use the Mini Translator

1 On the ribbon, click the Review tab.

2 Click Translate.

3 Click Mini Translator.

4 Drag to select the text you want to translate.

5 Hover the pointer over the text. When you see the Microsoft Translator toolbar, move the pointer onto the toolbar so that you can read the translation.

6 Click Copy.

7 Right-click in the OneNote page and choose a Paste option on the shortcut menu to paste the translation into a note.

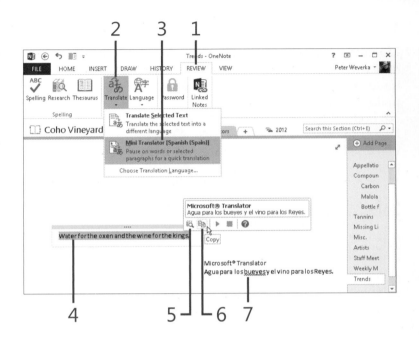

Finding the right word by using the Thesaurus

Sometimes it's difficult to find a word that says exactly what you mean to say. If this happens to you, consider giving the Thesaurus a try.

The Thesaurus offers synonyms for any word you select, in a tidy list on the Thesaurus task pane. If you find the right word in the list of synonyms, you can insert it into your note and instantly replace your original word.

If the Thesaurus does not initially show you a synonym that you want to use, you can continue to search for more synonyms.

Find the right word by using the Thesaurus

1 Drag to select a word.

2 On the ribbon, click the Review tab.

3 Click Thesaurus.

   The Thesaurus task pane opens on the right side of the screen.

4 Click a word in the synonyms list to look for synonyms of that word. (You might do this if you don't initially find the word that you are looking for.)

5 Right-click a word in the synonyms list and choose Insert to replace the selected word with the synonym from the Thesaurus.

6 Click Close on the Thesaurus task pane.

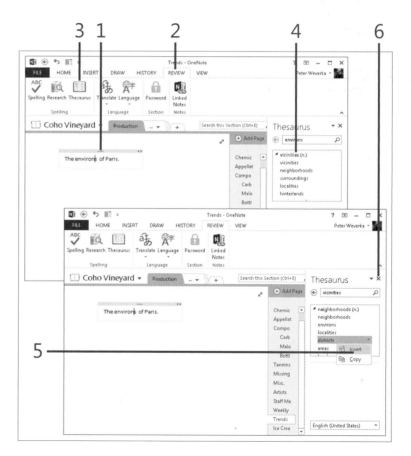

 TIP You can also open the Thesaurus by pressing Shift+F7.

 TIP You can also find a synonym for a word by using the Research task pane if it happens to be open. With the word for which you want to find a synonym selected, on the Services list, click Thesaurus.

Distributing your notes

To distribute notes, you can print them, send them by email, and save them in many common file formats, including PDF, XPS, and MHT. Distributing notes in a different format is a good way to share them with people who don't have OneNote.

Microsoft OneNote 2013 offers a special command for transferring a notebook from one computer to another. A OneNote notebook is composed of section files. Rather than meticulously copying all of the section files that make up a notebook, you can save your notebook in a special file and then simply open this file on the other computer.

In this section:

- Printing pages or an entire section
- Sending a page by email
- Exporting pages, sections, and notebooks in alternative file formats
- Transferring a notebook to another computer

Printing pages or an entire section

Using the standard Print command, you can print all or some of the pages in a section. The Print dialog box offers options for printing all the pages in a section, pages you select (select the pages before giving the Print command), or specific pages and page ranges.

Before you print a section, you can see what it will look like on the printed page. In the Print Preview And Settings dialog box, you can choose what size paper on which to print, resize data to fit exactly on the page, put page numbers on the pages you print, and print in landscape or portrait mode.

Print pages or an entire section

1 Click the section tab (or the section name in the Notebooks pane) with the pages that you want to print.

2 Select pages (by Ctrl+clicking if you want to print some but not all of the pages in the section. (If you don't select pages first, you can enter a page range to print later.)

3 On the ribbon, click the File tab to display the Backstage view.

4 Click the Print tab.

5 Click the Print button.

The Print dialog box opens.

6 Choose how many copies to print.

7 Choose All to print all the pages in a section. Choose Selection to print the pages you selected. Choose Pages and type the page range to print individual pages and page ranges without selecting them first.

8 Click Print.

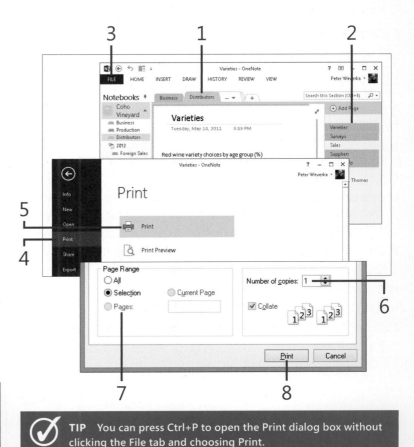

TIP To enter a page range, type the first page in the range, a hyphen, and then last page. Use commas to separate pages or page ranges. For example, enter 4-6 to print pages 4, 5, and 6, or 3,5,7-9 to print pages 3, 5, 7, 8, and 9.

TIP You can press Ctrl+P to open the Print dialog box without clicking the File tab and choosing Print.

Preview a section before printing

1 Click the section tab (or the section name in the Notebooks pane) that you want to preview.

You can select specific pages to preview if you want.

2 On the ribbon, click the File tab to display the Backstage view.

3 Click the Print tab.

4 Click the Print Preview button.

The Print Preview And Settings dialog box opens.

5 Click the Next Page (or Previous Page) button to examine different pages.

6 Open the Page Range list and choose to print a section, page group (a page and its subpages), or the current page.

7 Open the Paper Size list and choose the dimensions for the paper on which you want to print.

8 Select the Scale Content To Paper Width check box to enlarge or reduce the pages you print, if necessary, so each page fits on a single page of paper.

9 Choose Landscape to change the page orientation so that the pages print across the length of the paper.

10 Open the Footer list and choose whether to print the section name, page number, or both at the bottom of every page.

11 Click Print if you decide, after previewing, to print the section or selected pages. Otherwise, click Close.

> **TIP** Select the Start Page Numbering At 1 check box after adding a footer, if you want the pages numbered beginning at 1, even if you are not printing the first page in a section.

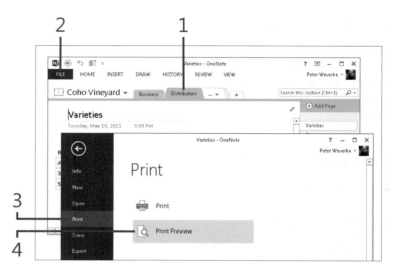

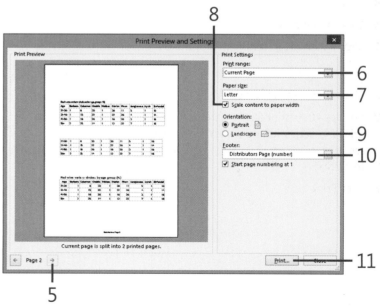

Sending a page by email

When you give a command to send a page by email, an Outlook 2013 message window opens automatically so that you can address the email message. You can write a message in the window to accompany the OneNote page. You can send a OneNote page in various formats, so even if your recipients don't have OneNote, they can still view the page.

OneNote offers three methods to send all the notes on a page by email:

- **Email page**   Send the notes on the page as text inside the email message. Use this method to send a page to someone who doesn't have OneNote.

- **Email as attachment**   Send the page as two file attachments. Using this technique, you send a section (.one) file and single file webpage (.mht) file. The recipient has the option of opening the .one file in OneNote and the .mht file in most web browsers. Use this method to send a page to someone who might not have OneNote.

- **Email page as PDF**   Send the page itself as an Adobe Portable Document Format (PDF) file. These files can be opened in Adobe Reader, a software program that most people have on their computers. Use this method to send the page to someone who doesn't have OneNote but wants to preserve the notes in a file and read them in Adobe Reader.

Send a page by email

1 In the page tabs, click the tab of the page that you want to send by email.

2 On the ribbon, click the File tab to display the Backstage view.

3 Click the Send tab.

4 Choose Email Page, Send As Attachment, or Send As PDF.

(continued on next page)

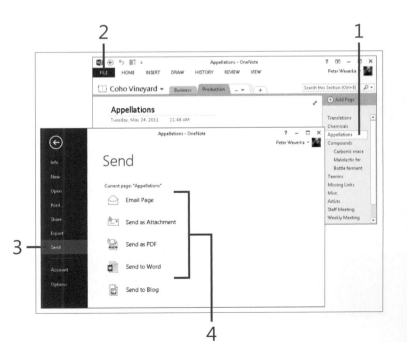

Send a page by email *(continued)*

5 Enter an email address in the message window.

6 Enter a message to accompany the attached files.

7 Click Send.

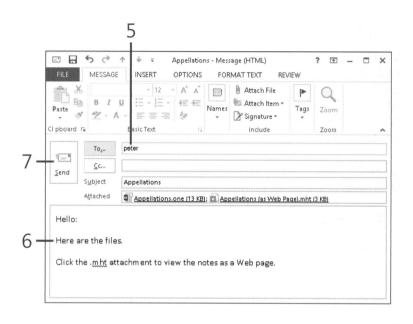

✓ **TIP** You can also email a page starting on the Home tab. Click the Email Page button to send the notes on the page as text inside an email message.

→ **TRY THIS** Send a OneNote page to yourself as an attachment. Then, after you receive your message, in the Outlook message window, double-click the .one file in the Attached box to see what happens when you send a .one file to a colleague. The .one file opens in OneNote. Double-click the .mht file to open the OneNote page in your browser.

Exporting pages, sections, and notebooks in alternative file formats

Export OneNote 2013 material in an alternative file format so that others who don't have OneNote can still read the material. OneNote offers a host of different ways to export pages, sections, and notebooks in alternative file formats.

After you give the Export command, you choose what to export (a page, section, or notebook). Then, you choose an alternative format for the file.

OneNote offers these export options:

Option	Exports	As
OneNote 2010-2013 section (.one)	A page or section	A OneNote 2010-2013 section file.
OneNote 2007 section (.one)	A page or section	A OneNote 2007 section file. Use this option for backward compatibility to give a page or section to someone running OneNote 2007.
Word document (.docx)	A page or section	A Microsoft Word document. The document can be read and edited in Word 2013, 2010, and 2007.
Word 97-2003 document (.doc)	A page or section	A Word 97-2003 document. The document can be read and edited in all versions of Word.
PDF (.pdf)	A page, section, or notebook	A Portable Document Format file. The file can be read in Adobe Reader, which is available on most computers.
XPS (.xps)	A page, section, or notebook	An XML Paper Specification file. The file can be read using XPS Viewer.
Single File Web Page (.mht)	A page or section	A Single File Web Page Format file. The file can be viewed in Internet Explorer and most other web browsers.
OneNote Package (.onepkg)	A notebook	A OneNote Package Format file. Choose this option to transfer a notebook from one computer to another.

Export a page, section, or notebook in an alternative file format

1 Open the page, section, or notebook that you want to export in a different format.

2 On the ribbon, click the File tab to display the Backstage view.

3 Click the Export tab.

4 Choose Page, Section, or Notebook.

5 Choose a file format.

6 Click Export.

The Save As dialog box opens.

7 Choose a folder in which to store the page, section, or notebook.

8 Click Save.

SEE ALSO To learn how to save a notebook as a OneNote Package file on your computer and open this file on a second computer, read "Transferring a notebook to another computer" on page 212.

Transferring a notebook to another computer

A OneNote 2013 notebook is composed of different section files (.one), one for each section. Because transferring all those section files to another computer would be difficult, OneNote provides a special file format for transferring notebooks between computers. The file format is called OneNote Package (*.onepkg).

To transfer a notebook to another computer, first save it as a OneNote Package file. Then, move or copy this file to the second computer and open it there. When you open the file, OneNote converts the OneNote Package file to a OneNote 2013 notebook.

Transfer a notebook to another computer

1 In the Notebooks pane, click the notebook that you want to transfer.

2 On the ribbon, click the File tab to display the Backstage view.

3 Click the Export tab.

4 Click Notebook.

5 Click OneNote Package (*.onepkg).

6 Click Export.

7 Choose a folder or disk for storing the OneNote package file.

8 Click Save.

(continued on next page)

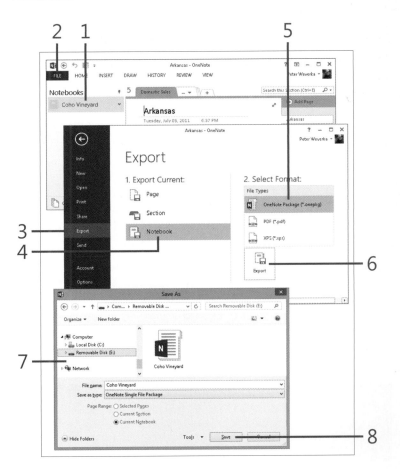

Transfer a notebook to another computer *(continued)*

9 Copy or move the file to the other computer.

10 On the other computer, in OneNote, click File.

11 Click Open.

12 Double-click Computer.

13 Open the File Type menu and choose OneNote Single File Package.

14 Choose the notebook you saved as a OneNote package file.

15 Click Open.

9 10   11   14

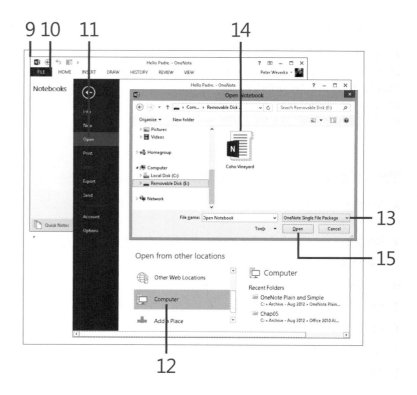

13

15

12

Using OneNote with other Office 2013 applications

16

Microsoft OneNote 2013 works hand in glove with Microsoft Word 2013 and Microsoft Outlook 2013.

In the case of Word, you can send a OneNote page to Word 2013. All formats except styles transfer to the Word page. After you edit the page in Word, you can save it as a Word document.

In the case of Outlook 2013, Outlook offers the OneNote button for copying email messages, contacts, and tasks directly from Outlook into OneNote. Moreover, when you copy a meeting, contact, or task, OneNote includes a link that you can click to return to Outlook when you need to.

In addition, you can create an Outlook task in OneNote without having to open Outlook. You can even mark the task as complete later on. You can copy information about a meeting directly from Outlook into OneNote, as well.

In this section:

- Sending a page to Word
- Copying Outlook items to OneNote
- Choosing how Outlook copies items to OneNote
- Creating an Outlook task in OneNote
- Changing or deleting an Outlook task in OneNote
- Copying meeting details from Outlook to a note

Sending a page to Word

OneNote 2013 offers a command for sending a page to Word. You can use this command to take advantage of the numerous editing tools that are available in Word and then save the page as a Word document. For example, if you take meeting notes or gather information for a report by using OneNote, you can later send the data to Word to create a professional-looking document.

When you send a page to Word, its formats are retained, but any OneNote styles in the page are not converted to Word styles. Also, although pictures, embedded spreadsheets, links, and the text of Outlook items are sent to Word, recorded audio and video are not.

Send a page to Word

1 Go to the page in OneNote that you want to open in Word. Make sure that the cursor is located on that page.

2 On the ribbon, click the File tab to display the Backstage view.

3 Click Send.

4 Click Send To Word.

   The page opens in Word. Use Word's tools to edit and save the page.

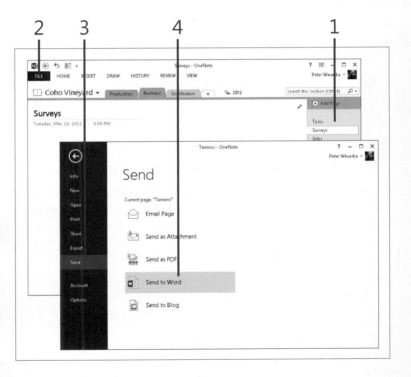

 TIP   To open several pages in Word, select page names on the page tabs in OneNote before giving the Send To Word command.

 SEE ALSO   To learn how to save entire sections or notebooks in Word format, read "Exporting pages, sections, and notebooks in alternative file formats" on page 210.

 SEE ALSO   To learn how to turn a OneNote table into a spreadsheet that you can edit with Excel, read "Converting a table into an Excel spreadsheet" on page 112.

Copying Outlook items to OneNote

In Outlook 2013, you can click the OneNote button to copy items from Outlook to OneNote. You can copy email messages, meetings, contacts, and tasks. Copy items from Outlook if you need to keep notes about email messages, meetings, contacts, or tasks.

In the case of meetings, contacts, and tasks, OneNote not only copies the item but it also provides a link that you can click to open the meeting, contact, or task in Outlook.

Copy an Outlook message, contact, or task to OneNote

1 Start Outlook.

2 Open the folder that contains the item you want to copy to OneNote.

3 Select the email message, contact, or task that you want to copy to OneNote.

4 On the ribbon, click the Home tab.

5 In the Actions group, click the OneNote button.

The Select Location In OneNote dialog box opens.

6 Select a section to create a new page for the item or select a page to copy the Outlook item to the page you selected. (Click the plus sign next to a section to display its pages.)

7 Click OK.

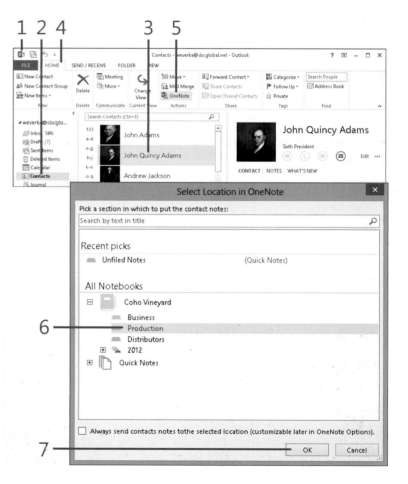

> ⚠ **CAUTION** When you copy an Outlook message to OneNote, a link is not created.

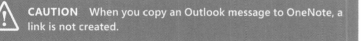

> ➔ **TRY THIS** When you copy an Outlook contact or task to OneNote, OneNote creates a link labeled Link To Outlook Item. Click this link in OneNote to open the item in Outlook. (To open a task in Outlook, right-click the Task flag and choose Open Task in Outlook.)

Copy an Outlook calendar item to OneNote

1 Start Outlook.

2 Open the folder with the item you want to copy to OneNote.

3 Select the calendar item that you want to copy to OneNote.

4 On the ribbon, click the Calendar Tools | Appointment, Appointment Series, Appointment Occurrence, or Meeting tab.

The tab that appears depends on the kind of calendar item you selected in step 3.

5 Also on the ribbon, click the Meeting Notes button.

6 In the drop-down list that appears, select Take Notes On Your Own.

The Select Location in OneNote dialog box opens.

7 Select a section to create a new page for the item. Select a page to copy the Outlook item to that page. (Click the plus sign next to a section to display its pages.)

8 Click OK.

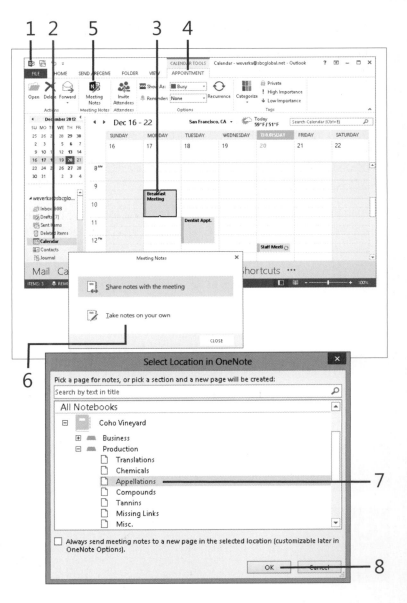

> ⚠️ **CAUTION** To open an item in Outlook, click its link. Changes you make are saved in Outlook, but do not appear in OneNote. Likewise, if you make changes to an item's information in OneNote, those changes do not affect Outlook.

> ✓ **TIP** When you copy a calendar item to OneNote, you are given an opportunity to share your meeting notes. To do so, in step 6, select Share Notes With The Meeting and then select a notebook you've already shared on SharePoint or your SkyDrive. In the calendar item, a link is added to the shared notebook. You can invite colleagues to your meeting and share the notebook with them through this link.

Choosing how Outlook copies items to OneNote

By default, when you copy Outlook 2013 items to OneNote 2013, the Select Location In OneNote dialog box opens, in which you can choose where to copy the items.

Rather than choose every time where in OneNote to copy an Outlook item, you can copy the item by default to the current page, a new page, or a default location of your choice. The options for copying Outlook items to OneNote are as follows:

- **Always Ask Where to Send**   The Select Location In OneNote dialog box opens. Here, you can send the Outlook item to a section of your choice. (This is the default option.)

- **To Current Page**   The Outlook item is copied to the currently opened page in OneNote.

- **To New Page In Current Section**   The Outlook item is copied to a new page in the currently opened section in OneNote.

- **Set Default Location**   The Outlook item is copied to a default section or page. In the Select Location In OneNote dialog box, choose the section or page that you want as the default and click OK.

Choose how Outlook copies items to OneNote

1 On the ribbon, click File to display the Backstage view.

2 Click Options.

The OneNote Options dialog box opens.

3 Click Send To OneNote.

4 Under Outlook Items, for email messages, meetings, contacts, and tasks, choose how you want to copy items to OneNote. If you choose Set Default Location, choose the section that you want as the default in the Select Location In OneNote dialog box and click OK.

5 Click OK once more.

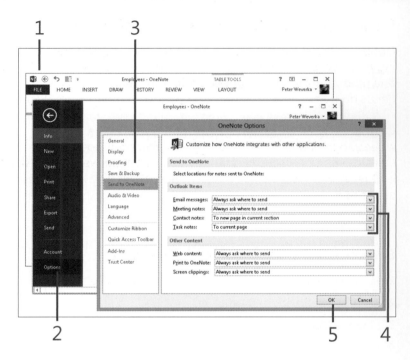

Creating an Outlook task in OneNote

Outlook 2013 offers the Tasks folder for recording and tracking tasks. When you create a task, you record its start date and due date. You can open the Tasks folder in Outlook to see what needs doing and when it's due, and plan your time accordingly.

OneNote 2013 gives you the opportunity to create a task without opening Outlook. The tasks are recorded both on a OneNote page and in Outlook. You can switch between the task in OneNote and the task in Outlook, and in this way keep notes about tasks.

To create an Outlook task in OneNote, start by writing a note that describes the task. The description doubles as a note and task name. For example, a note with the text "Gather data for emerging market analysis" is recorded in the Outlook Tasks folder as this task: "Gather data for emerging market analysis." After you write the note, you change it into an Outlook task by choosing a due date for the task.

In OneNote, tasks are marked with the task icon (a red flag). You can make changes to a task in OneNote and even open the OneNote task from Outlook.

Create an Outlook task in OneNote

1 In OneNote, click the note that you want to create as a task.

2 On the ribbon, click the Home tab.

3 Click the Outlook Tasks button.

4 Choose a due date for the task.

The task is created in OneNote and Outlook. A task flag indicating the due date appears to the left of the note.

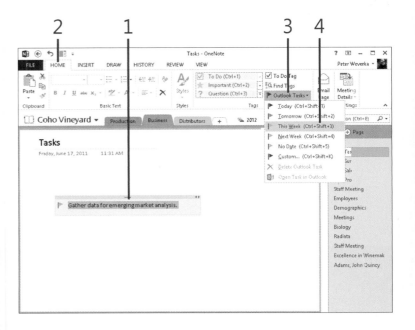

→ TRY THIS Right-click a task icon (the flag) and choose a different due date to quickly change the due date of a task.

⊙ SEE ALSO To learn how to manage Outlook tasks in OneNote read "Changing or deleting an Outlook task in OneNote" on page 223.

Open a OneNote task from Outlook

1 Start Outlook.

2 Open the Tasks folder.

3 Double-click the task that you created in OneNote to open it in a Task window.

4 Double-click the Link To Task In OneNote link to open the OneNote page where the task was created and take notes on the task.

Changing or deleting an Outlook task in OneNote

You can create an Outlook 2013 task in OneNote 2013, or copy an existing task from Outlook to OneNote. You can change and delete Outlook tasks copied or created in OneNote, as well. In OneNote, manage Outlook tasks with these techniques:

- **Mark a task as complete** Tasks that are marked as complete show the check mark icon, not the red flag.

- **Delete a task** Delete a task when it is complete and, furthermore, you don't need a record of having completed it.

- **Change the due date** Change the due date to today, tomorrow, this week, next week, or a custom date that you select. You can also remove the due date associated with a task if it has no due date.

Change or delete an Outlook task in OneNote

1 Click the task that you want to change or delete.

2 On the ribbon, click the Home tab.

3 Click Outlook Tasks.

4 Choose a new due date for the task or choose No Date to remove the due date. If you choose Custom, the Task window opens; select a due date and click Save & Close.

5 Right-click the task icon and choose Mark Complete to check off the task as "done."

6 Right-click the task icon and choose Delete Outlook Task to delete the task permanently.

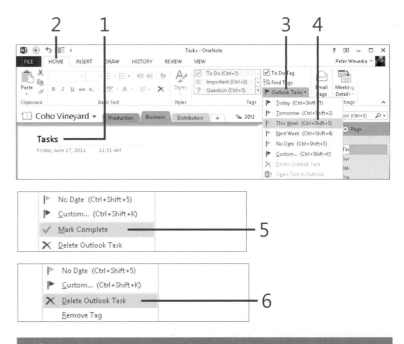

> ✓ **TIP** Quickly change the due date of a task by selecting the task and pressing Ctrl+Shift+1 (Today), Ctrl+Shift+2 (Tomorrow), Ctrl+Shift+3 (This Week), Ctrl+Shift+4 (Next Week), or Ctrl+Shift+K (Custom).

> ⚠ **CAUTION** If you select No Date for a task, Outlook places the task at the top of the tasks list, above tasks due Today. For this reason, it's best to select a date for every task so that they can be sorted correctly.

> ⚠ **CAUTION** If you delete a task in OneNote, its task flag is removed but the text remains. You can delete the text manually if you like. Moreover, when you delete a task in OneNote, the task is removed completely from Outlook.

Copying meeting details from Outlook to a note

Using the Calendar, you can schedule meetings in Outlook 2013. When you schedule a meeting, you enter its name, date and time, and, if you want, a description.

OneNote 2013 offers the Meeting Details command to copy meeting details from Outlook into a note. The details appear in a table. Below the table, you can write your thoughts about the meeting and in so doing, prepare yourself for it. You can also take notes during the meeting.

To transfer details about a meeting into a note, click the Meeting Details button. In the gallery that appears, you can copy details about meetings scheduled for today, past days, and future days.

Copy meeting details from Outlook to a note

1 On the ribbon, click the Home tab.

2 Click the Meeting Details button.

3 Select a meeting from the Today's Meetings list or click Choose A Meeting From Another Day.

The Insert Outlook Meeting Details dialog box appears.

4 Click the Calendar button and select a day to display scheduled meetings on that day.

5 Select a meeting.

6 Click Insert Details.

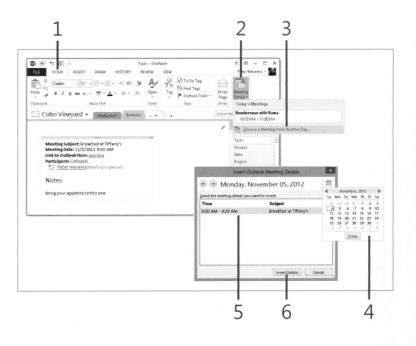

TIP You can click the Previous Day or Next Day buttons in the Insert Outlook Meeting Details dialog box to locate a meeting, rather than click the Calendar button.

TRY THIS Insert a recent meeting in a OneNote page. Notice the space below the meeting details for writing notes about the meeting. Enter some notes there.

SEE ALSO To learn how to send meeting details to OneNote by starting in Outlook, read "Copying Outlook items to OneNote" on page 217.

Sharing notebooks with others

17

Microsoft OneNote 2013 offers the History tab to help you collaborate with others on a shared notebook. On the tab are commands for finding out who wrote different notes, marking pages with notes you haven't read yet, marking pages that you have read, and finding notes written in your absence.

Sharing notebooks is a great way to pool resources and share information with colleagues, coworkers, or fellow students.

In this section:

- Sharing a notebook
- Synchronizing shared notebooks
- Finding unread notes
- Finding notes by specific authors
- Finding recently edited notes

Sharing a notebook

You can share OneNote 2013 notebooks on a network, in a folder on SkyDrive, or on a Microsoft SharePoint website:

- If your computer is connected to a network, you can share OneNote notebooks on a shared network folder. To do that, you must save or move the notebook to the shared folder.

- SkyDrive is an online service from Microsoft for storing and sharing files. To use SkyDrive, you need to sign up for a Microsoft Account (it's free). You can share notebooks with other Microsoft Account users by placing notebooks in a SkyDrive folder.

- Microsoft SharePoint is a software product designed to help people share files. Users can share OneNote notebooks on a SharePoint website.

Sharing a notebook entails moving it to a location where others can access it. OneNote synchronizes the version of the notebook on your computer or tablet and the one on a network or the Internet.

Share a notebook on SharePoint

1 On the ribbon, click the File tab to display the Backstage view.

2 Click the Share tab.

3 Choose the SharePoint location where you want to share your notebook.

4 Click Browse.

(continued on next page)

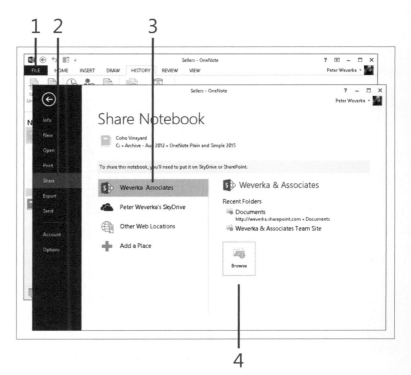

Share a notebook on SharePoint *(continued)*

5 In the Move Notebook dialog box, choose a folder.

6 Click Open.

5

6

TIP To share a notebook when you create it, select a network or web location in the New Notebook window.

TIP To discontinue sharing a notebook, click File, click Info, and then, in the Notebook Information window, click the Settings button and choose Properties from the drop-down list. Then, in the Notebook Properties dialog box, click the Change Location button, and in the dialog box that appears, select a folder that is not shared.

Share a notebook on SkyDrive

1 On the ribbon, click the File tab to display the Backstage view.

2 Click the Share tab.

3 Choose the SkyDrive location where you want to share your notebook.

4 Click Move Notebook.

5 Click OK in the pop-up message box that says your notebook is synching to the new location.

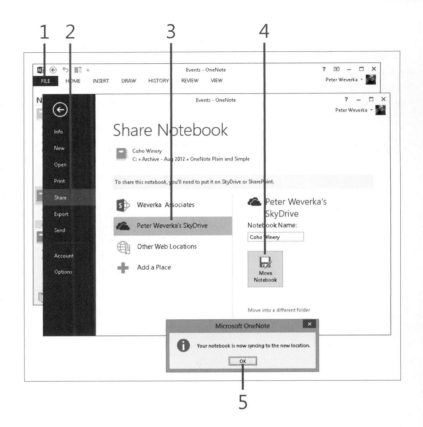

SEE ALSO   To learn how to share and collaborate with others on SkyDrive by using OneNote Web App, read "Inviting others to share a notebook on SkyDrive" on page 257.

Synchronizing shared notebooks

OneNote 2013 synchronizes notebooks that you share with others so that the version of the notebook on your computer or device and the version on a network, SkyDrive, or SharePoint are identical. By default, synchronizing is done automatically,

behind the scenes. You can, however, synchronize a notebook whenever you want. You can also sync all notebooks manually, at a time of your choosing. At any time, you can check when OneNote last synchronized your shared notebooks.

Synchronize shared notebooks

1 On the ribbon, click the File tab to display the Backstage view.

2 Click the Info tab.

3 Click View Sync Status.

4 In the Shared Notebook Synchronization dialog box, notice when your notebooks were last synchronized (click the Sync Now button to synchronize a notebook right away).

5 Click Sync All to synchronize all your shared notebooks.

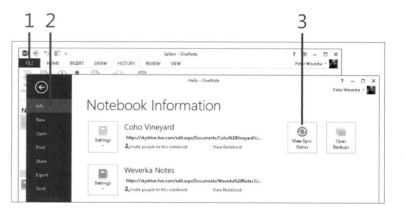

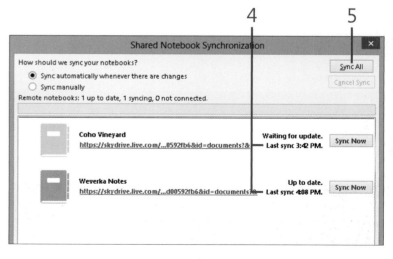

> **TIP** Press F9 to synchronize all your notebooks at any time. Press Shift+F9 to synchronize only the notebook that is currently open.

> **TIP** If you prefer to synchronize your notebooks on your own, open the Shared Notebook Synchronization dialog box and choose the Sync Manually option. Then, to synchronize your notebooks, open the dialog box and click the Sync All button (or the Sync Now button for individual notebooks).

Finding unread notes

When you open a OneNote 2013 notebook that you share with others, notes written by others since the previous time you opened the notebook are highlighted. What's more, in the page tabs, the names of pages with unread notes appear in bold letters.

OneNote offers tools to help you keep track of which pages you've read in a shared notebook and which pages you haven't read. As you view a page, the notes on it are marked as read,

and the highlight is removed from the page name. In addition, the bold style is removed from the name of the page on the page tabs. You can mark notes on a page as unread so that you can remember to revisit them later.

Sometimes, notes are not marked as read because the changes were made by you on another device. If that happens, you can mark pages as read so that you know they have been reviewed.

Find unread notes

1   On the ribbon, click the History tab.

2   Click Next Unread to go to the next page that has notes that have not been read.

3   Hover the pointer over an author's initials. In the ScreenTip that appears, note the author's name and note modification date.

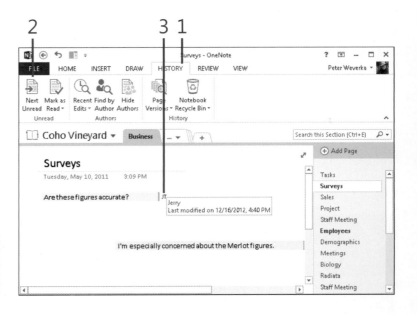

> ✓ **TIP**   If unread notes are not highlighted, and the names of pages with unread notes are not bold in the page tabs, click the Mark As Read button and choose Show Unread Changes In This Notebook.

> ⚠ **CAUTION**   If authors' initials don't appear, on the History tab, click the Hide Authors button to display them. (The Hide Authors button is a toggle.)

Finding notes by specific authors

Notes are marked with their authors' initials (if they do not appear to be marked, on the History tab, click Hide Authors to display author initials). When you move the pointer over these initials, a ScreenTip appears with the author's name and the date when she wrote the note.

In shared notebooks, OneNote 2013 keeps track of who wrote each note. You can find notes from specific authors by using the Find By Author command.

Find notes by a specific author

1 On the ribbon, click the History tab.

2 In the Authors group, click Find By Author.

3 In the Search Results pane, click an author's name.

4 Click a page name to view its contents.

> **TIP** To see past versions of a page from other authors, on the History tab, click the Page Versions button and then, in the drop-down list that appears, choose Page Versions. In the page tabs, page versions by other authors show the other authors' names. See "Revisiting and restoring a different version of a page" on page 49 to learn the details about using the Page Versions command.

> **CAUTION** To mark notes, OneNote gets author names and initials from the OneNote Options dialog box. Make sure your name and initials are entered correctly in this dialog box. Click the File button. Then, in the Backstage view, click the Options tab. In the OneNote Options dialog box, in the General category, enter your user name and initials.

Finding recently edited notes

One way to search for notes that you haven't read is to show only notes in a specific timeframe. For example, you can direct OneNote to show only notes written or edited in the past week. In this way, you can focus on notes that matter to you.

The History tab offers the Recent Edits button for finding notes by timeframe.

Find recently edited notes

1 On the ribbon, click the History tab.

2 In the Authors group, click Recent Edits.

3 On the menu that appears, click a timeframe.

4 Click a page name to view its contents.

TIP Click the Recent Edits button and choose All Pages Sorted by date to get a list of all pages and the dates on which they were last edited in the Search Results task pane.

SEE ALSO To learn how to search different parts of a notebook with the Search Results pane, read "Searching a section, section group, or notebook" on page 175.

Customizing OneNote 2013

Except by pressing keyboard shortcuts, you give commands in OneNote 2013 by using the ribbon and the Quick Access Toolbar. To make using OneNote easier, you can customize both.

You can place the commands you use most often and the commands you find most useful on the ribbon and Quick Access Toolbar. You can also remove commands, rearrange commands, and, in the case of the ribbon, create your own tabs and command groups on tabs. If you want, you can place the Quick Access Toolbar below the ribbon rather than above it.

If you discover after you customize the Quick Access Toolbar or ribbon that you want the original back, you can revert to it easily. OneNote offers Reset commands for restoring them both to their default settings.

In this section:

- Adding or removing Quick Access Toolbar buttons
- Changing the order of buttons on the Quick Access Toolbar
- Repositioning the Quick Access Toolbar
- Resetting the Quick Access Toolbar
- Customizing the ribbon
- Creating or removing a ribbon tab
- Creating or removing a ribbon group
- Adding or removing commands from a ribbon group
- Renaming a ribbon tab or group
- Moving a ribbon tab or group
- Resetting your ribbon customizations

Adding or removing Quick Access Toolbar buttons

For your convenience, the Quick Access Toolbar appears in the upper-left corner of the OneNote window in Normal view. This toolbar offers a handful of useful buttons: Back, Undo, and Dock To Desktop (and if you have a tablet, the Touch/Mouse Mode button, to switch to Touch mode). The commands on the Quick Access Toolbar are easy to access.

OneNote 2013 offers the capability to add more buttons to and remove buttons from the Quick Access Toolbar so that you can include the buttons that you use most often.

Add Quick Access Toolbar buttons

1 On the Quick Access Toolbar, click the Customize Quick Access Toolbar button.

2 On the menu that appears, click More Commands.

(continued on next page)

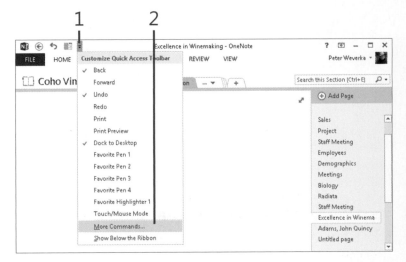

Add Quick Access Toolbar buttons *(continued)*

3 In the OneNote Options dialog box, in the Choose Commands From list box, choose All Commands or a subset of commands to display.

4 In the list of commands on the left, choose the command that you want to add to the Quick Access Toolbar.

5 Click Add.

6 Click OK.

> **TIP** Click the Customize Quick Access Toolbar button and then, from the drop-down list that appears, choose a button name to quickly add a button to the toolbar.

Remove Quick Access Toolbar buttons

1 On the Quick Access Toolbar, right-click the button that you want to remove.

2 On the shortcut menu that appears, click Remove From Quick Access Toolbar.

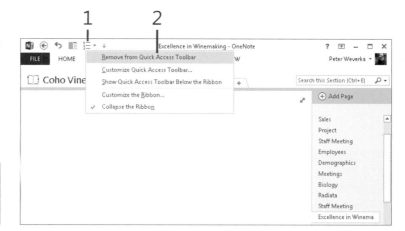

> **SEE ALSO** To learn how to reset the Quick Access Toolbar to its default settings, read "Resetting the Quick Access Toolbar" on page 238.

Changing the order of buttons on the Quick Access Toolbar

You can change the order of the buttons on the OneNote 2013 Quick Access Toolbar to place them where they're most convenient for you. Especially if you've placed many buttons on the toolbar, changing the order can help you locate buttons.

Change the order of buttons on the Quick Access Toolbar

1 On the Quick Access Toolbar, click the Customize Quick Access Toolbar button.

2 On the menu that appears, click More Commands.

3 Select the button for which you want to change the order.

4 Click the Move Up (or Move Down) button as many times as necessary to place the button where you want it to be.

5 Click OK.

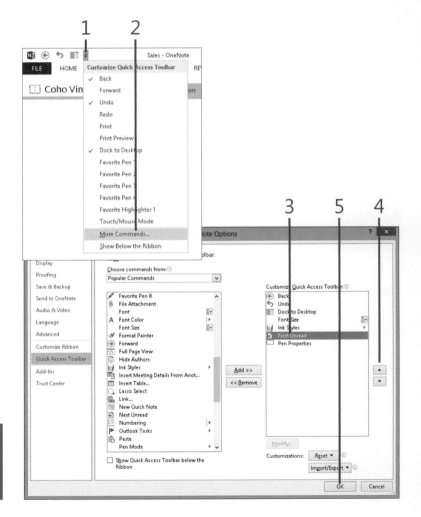

TIP You can also open the Quick Access Toolbar tab of the OneNote Options dialog box by clicking the File tab, choosing the Options tab in the Backstage view, and then choosing Quick Access Toolbar.

Repositioning the Quick Access Toolbar

The Quick Access Toolbar in OneNote 2013 can become too crowded with buttons. In that case, consider moving it below the ribbon, where there is enough room to comfortably display a dozen or more buttons.

Reposition the Quick Access Toolbar below the ribbon

1 On the Quick Access Toolbar, click the Customize Quick Access Toolbar button.

2 On the menu that appears, click Show Below The Ribbon.

Reposition the Quick Access Toolbar above the ribbon

1 On the Quick Access Toolbar, click the Customize Quick Access Toolbar button.

2 On the menu that appears, click Show Above The Ribbon.

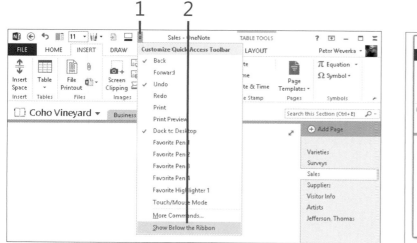

TIP You can also reposition the Quick Access Toolbar by right-clicking the toolbar and then, on the shortcut menu that appears, clicking Show Below The Ribbon or Show Above The Ribbon.

Resetting the Quick Access Toolbar

Reset the Quick Access Toolbar to remove all of your customizations. Only the three or four default buttons—Back, Undo, and Dock To Desktop (and Touch/Mouse Mode, in the case of tablets)—remain on the Quick Access Toolbar after

you reset it. Resetting the Quick Access Toolbar to its default settings doesn't move it above the ribbon if you happened to have moved it below. Resetting applies only to the buttons on the toolbar, not the toolbar's location.

Reset the Quick Access Toolbar

1 On the Quick Access Toolbar, click the Customize Quick Access Toolbar button.

2 On the menu that appears, click More Commands.

3 In the OneNote Option dialog box, click Reset. On the menu that appears, click Reset Only Quick Access Toolbar.

4 In the pop-up message box, click Yes to confirm.

5 Click OK.

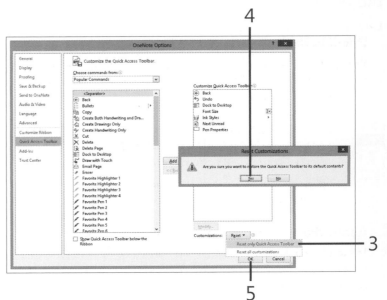

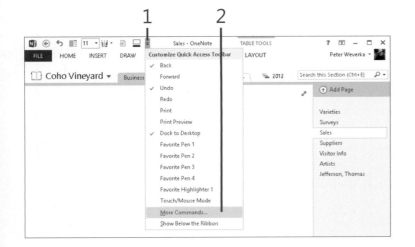

Customizing the ribbon

The ribbon is the stretch of ground across the top of the OneNote 2013 window. It is composed of different tabs, and on each tab are commands divided into groups. To undertake a task, you click a tab on the ribbon, look for the group with the commands you need, and then choose commands.

To get more out of OneNote, you can customize the ribbon. You can create your own tabs, and within those tabs, you can set up your own groups, which you can populate with commands of your choice. Moreover, you can rename tabs and groups; change the order of tabs on the ribbon; and within each tab, change the order of command groups.

Opening the Customize The Ribbon dialog box

To customize the ribbon, start by opening the Customize The Ribbon window in the OneNote Options dialog box. Use one of these techniques to open this window:

- Click the File tab to display the Backstage view and then click the Options tab. Then, in the OneNote Options dialog box, click the Customize Ribbon tab.

- Right-click the ribbon and then, on the shortcut menu that appears, click Customize The Ribbon.

About the Customize The Ribbon dialog box

The left side of the Customize The Ribbon dialog box lists OneNote commands. To locate a command to work with, choose a subset of commands on the Choose Commands From menu (or choose All Commands). For example, to find a command that you know is on the Draw tab, click Main Tabs on the Choose Commands From menu, and then click the expand button next to the Draw tab to display its commands.

The right side of the Customize The Ribbon dialog box shows the names of tabs. Within each tab are the names of groups, and within each group are the names of commands currently on the ribbon. To display the name of a tab, group, or the commands within groups, click the expand button next to a tab name or group name.

Choose Commands From menu

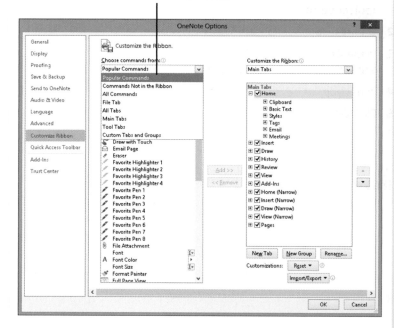

Creating or removing a ribbon tab

You can create a new tab for the ribbon and then load it with your favorite commands. You can also remove a tab that you created and added to the ribbon. You cannot remove the tabs that you didn't create.

When you create a new tab, OneNote creates a new group to go with it. Your next task after creating a new tab is to rename the group that came with it and populate your new tab with groups and commands.

Create a ribbon tab

1 Right-click anywhere on the ribbon. On the shortcut menu that appears, click Customize The Ribbon.

2 In the Customize The Ribbon window of the OneNote Options dialog box, in the Customize The Ribbon section on the right, select the tab that your new tab will follow.

For example, to create a new tab to the right of the History tab, select History.

3 Click New Tab.

OneNote creates a new tab and new group for the tab.

4 Select the tab you created (it's called New Tab [Custom]).

5 Click Rename.

6 In the Rename dialog box, enter a name for the new tab. Default tabs are labeled with capital letters, but you don't have to use capital letters if you don't want to.

7 Click OK to save the name and close the Rename dialog box.

8 Click OK to save the settings and close the OneNote Options dialog box.

> **SEE ALSO** To learn how to restore the default ribbon, read "Resetting your ribbon customizations" on page 248.

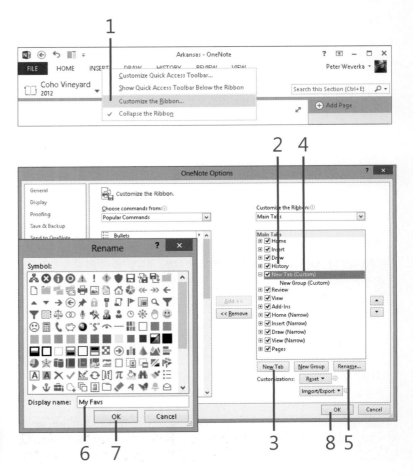

Remove a ribbon tab

1 Right-click anywhere on the ribbon. On the shortcut menu that appears, click Customize The Ribbon.

2 In the Customize The Ribbon window of the OneNote Options dialog box, in the Customize The Ribbon section on the right, right-click the custom tab that you want to remove.

3 On the shortcut menu that appears, click Remove.

4 Click OK.

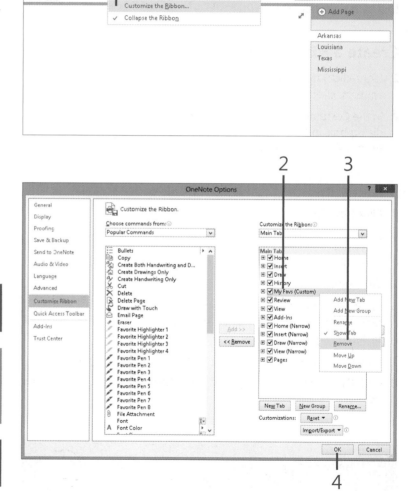

SEE ALSO To learn how to create groups within tabs on the ribbon, read "Creating or removing a ribbon group" on page 242.

⚠️ CAUTION You can only remove tabs from the ribbon that you created yourself. You can hide a default tab, however, by clearing the check box adjacent to its name in the Customize The Ribbon dialog box.

SEE ALSO To learn how to restore the default ribbon, read "Resetting your ribbon customizations" on page 248.

Creating or removing a ribbon group

Within each tab on the OneNote 2013 ribbon are different groups of commands. For example, the Home tab has six groups: Clipboard, Basic Text, Styles, Tags, Email, and Meetings. Commands of similar purpose are grouped on a tab to make locating them easier. You can create a new group on any tab, not just tabs that you create yourself. Create a new group so that you can place commands in it later on.

If you no longer need a group, you can remove it from a tab. When you remove a group, you remove its buttons, as well. You can remove any group, even a default group.

Create a ribbon group

1. Right-click anywhere on the ribbon. On the shortcut menu that appears, click Customize the Ribbon.

2. In the Customize The Ribbon window of the OneNote Options dialog box, in the Customize The Ribbon section on the right, click the expand button next to the tab into which the new group will go.

3. Select the group that your new group will follow.

4. Click New Group. OneNote creates a group called "New Group (Custom)."

5. Click Rename.

6. In the Rename dialog box, enter a name and click OK.

7. Click OK to save the settings and close the OneNote Options dialog box.

> **SEE ALSO** To learn how to add commands to a ribbon group that you created, read "Adding or removing commands from a ribbon group" on page 244.

> **SEE ALSO** To learn how to restore the default ribbon, read "Resetting your ribbon customizations" on page 248.

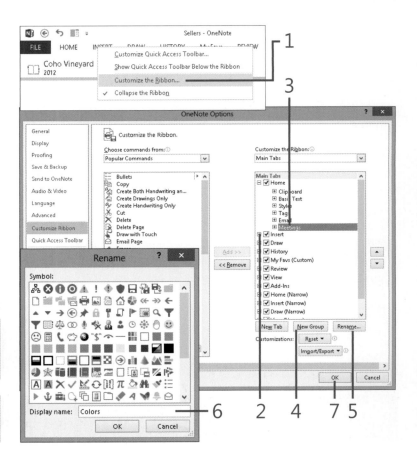

Remove a ribbon group

1 Right-click anywhere on the ribbon. On the shortcut menu that appears, click Customize The Ribbon.

2 In the Customize The Ribbon window of the OneNote Options dialog box, in the Customize The Ribbon section on the right, click the expand button next to the name of the tab that holds the group you want to remove.

You see a list of groups on the tab.

3 Select the group that you want to remove.

4 Right-click the group and then, on the shortcut menu that appears, click Remove.

5 Click OK to remove the group, along with its commands, from the ribbon.

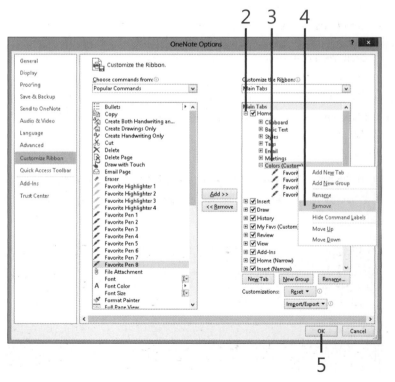

> ⚠ **CAUTION** If you accidentally removed a default group that you wanted to keep, you can reset the tab to bring it back.

Adding or removing commands from a ribbon group

Add commands to a ribbon group to assemble commands that you find most useful in one place. OneNote keeps a list of all its commands in the Customize The Ribbon section of the OneNote Options dialog box. You can add any command you want to a custom group that you created.

Remove commands from a group if you find that you don't use them. You can only remove commands from a custom group that you created.

Add commands to a ribbon group

1 Right-click any tab name on the ribbon. On the shortcut menu that appears, click Customize The Ribbon.

2 In the Customize The Ribbon window of the OneNote Options dialog box, in the Choose Commands From section on the left, select a command to add to the group (if you have trouble finding a command, open the menu and choose a subset of commands or All Commands).

3 In the Customize The Ribbon section, click the expand button next to a tab to see its command groups.

4 Select the name of a custom group that you created.

5 Click Add.

6 Click OK.

> **→ TRY THIS** Select a command and click Move Up or Move Down to change its position in a group.

> **✓ TIP** While the Customize The Ribbon dialog box is open, you can add as many commands as you please to the ribbon before clicking OK.

> **⊙ SEE ALSO** To learn how to create a ribbon group for your favorite commands, read "Creating or removing a ribbon group" on page 242.

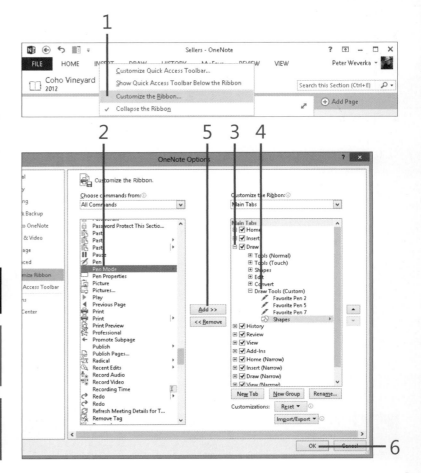

Remove commands from a ribbon group

1 Right-click anywhere on the ribbon. On the shortcut menu that appears, click Customize The Ribbon.

2 In the Customize The Ribbon window of the OneNote Options dialog box, in the Customize The Ribbon section on the right, click the expand button next to the tab with the command that you want to remove.

3 Click the expand button next to the group with the command that you want to remove.

4 Select the name of the command to remove.

5 Click Remove.

6 Click OK.

1

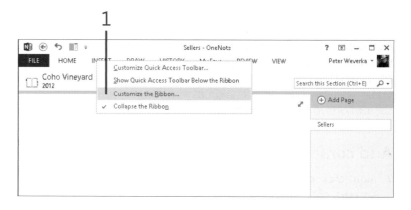

5 2 3 4

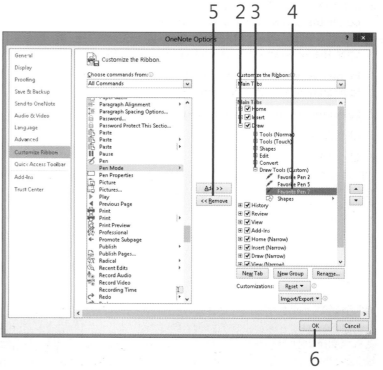

 TIP You can leave the OneNote Options dialog box open and remove several commands before closing it.

⚠ **CAUTION** You can only remove commands from a custom group. You can, however, remove an entire group from a default tab.

6

Renaming a ribbon tab or group

Are some ribbon tabs and group names not descriptive enough for you? You can rename ribbon tabs and groups and give them names that make it easier for you to recognize them and locate the commands they offer. You can rename any tab or group.

Rename a ribbon tab or group

1 Right-click any tab name on the ribbon. On the shortcut menu that appears, click Customize The Ribbon.

2 In the Customize The Ribbon window of the OneNote Options dialog box, in the Customize The Ribbon section on the right, select the ribbon tab or group that you want to rename. To see a group, click the expand button next to the tab with the group you want to rename.

3 Click Rename.

4 In the Rename dialog box, enter a new name and click OK.

5 In the OneNote Options dialog box, click OK.

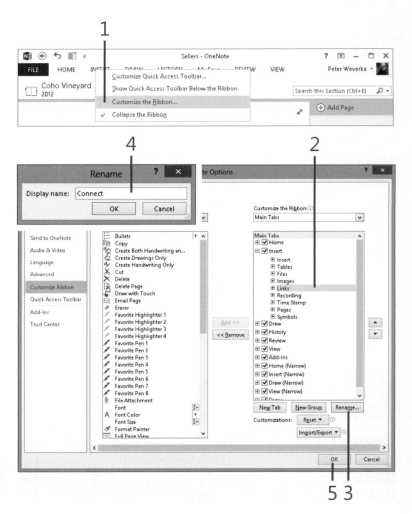

SEE ALSO To learn how to restore the default ribbon, read "Resetting your ribbon customizations" on page 248.

Moving a ribbon tab or group

Move ribbon tabs to make them easier to find on the ribbon. You can also move ribbon groups to make them easier to find on a tab.

Move a ribbon tab or group

1 Click the File tab to display the Backstage view.

2 Click the Options tab.

3 In the Outlook Options dialog box, click the Customize Ribbon tab.

4 In the Customize The Ribbon section, select the tab or group that you want to relocate.

5 Click Move Up or Move Down as many times as necessary to move the tab or group to the desired location.

6 Click OK.

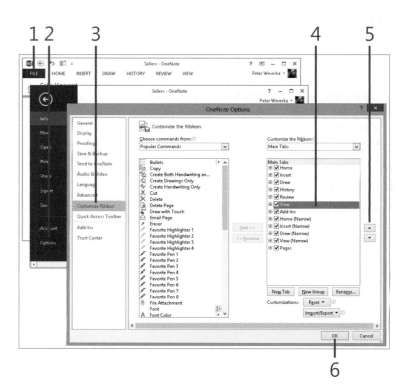

SEE ALSO To learn how to create a ribbon group for your favorite commands, read "Creating or removing a ribbon group" on page 242.

Resetting your ribbon customizations

If you make a hash of the OneNote 2013 ribbon and want to start over, you can reset your customizations. By resetting your customizations, you get the default ribbon back, but you lose any new tabs, groups, or commands that you added to the ribbon.

Reset your ribbon customizations

1 Right-click anywhere on the ribbon. On the shortcut menu that appears, click Customize the Ribbon.

2 In the Customize The Ribbon window of the OneNote Options dialog box, in the Customize The Ribbon section, click Reset.

3 On the menu that appears, click Reset All Customizations.

4 In the pop-up message box asking to confirm the deletion, click Yes.

5 Click OK.

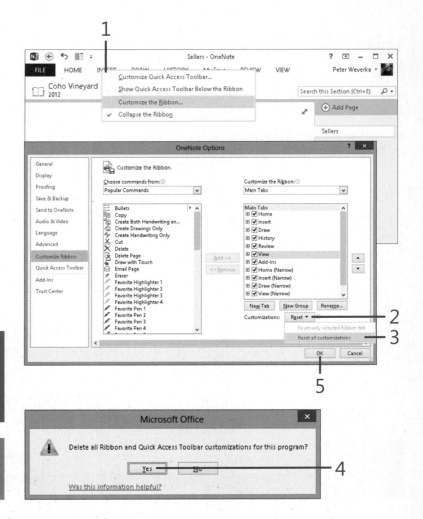

> ✓ **TIP** You can also reset only the customizations you made to a particular tab on the ribbon. Select a tab name on the right side of the Customize The Ribbon dialog box, click Reset, and then choose Reset Only Selected Ribbon tab (or right-click the tab name and choose Reset Tab).

> ⚠ **CAUTION** Resetting all customizations on the ribbon also resets any customizations that you made to the Quick Access Toolbar.

Using OneNote Web App

Anyone can use OneNote Web App, the online version of Microsoft OneNote 2013. You don't have to pay a fee or even install Microsoft Office 2013 on your computer. All you need is an Internet connection and a Microsoft Account (formerly Windows Live ID).

OneNote Web App is an abridged version of OneNote 2013. It doesn't offer as many commands, but it does offer an excellent opportunity to coauthor notebooks with others. Because the notebooks are kept online, not on someone's computer, anyone with an Internet connection and a Microsoft Account can access their own notebooks and notebooks that others have shared with them. Hundreds of people can coauthor a single shared notebook. What's more, they can work on a notebook at the same time, and if they need a command that isn't in OneNote Web App, they can open the file in OneNote and edit it there.

You can share notebooks on SkyDrive, a free file-hosting service from Microsoft, or on Microsoft Office 365, a subscription-based service from Microsoft that provides either storage capacity on SkyDrive or a Share-Point team site designed for collaboration.

In this section:

- Getting ready to use OneNote Web App
- Creating SkyDrive folders for storing notebooks
- Creating a notebook in SkyDrive
- Opening a notebook in OneNote
- Inviting others to share a notebook on SkyDrive
- Finding out who made changes to a SkyDrive notebook
- Creating a notebook in Office 365

Getting ready to use OneNote Web App

OneNote Web App is the online version of OneNote 2013 that you use through your web browser to edit notebooks stored on SkyDrive or an Office 365 team site (SharePoint site). OneNote Web App offers many, but not all, of the commands in OneNote. However, if you can't find the command you need in OneNote Web App, you can open your notebook in OneNote, work on it there, and save it to the SkyDrive or SharePoint folder where your notebook is stored.

A notebook in OneNote Web App

The same notebook in OneNote 2013

To use OneNote Web App on SkyDrive (and to share notebooks with others if you want), you need a Microsoft Account (formerly called Windows Live ID). Having a Microsoft Account entitles you to web-based applications (such as OneNote Web App) and services such as SkyDrive for storing and sharing OneNote notebooks.

You can edit notebooks stored on SkyDrive or an Office 365 SharePoint team site by using OneNote Web App, OneNote, or OneNote Mobile. Because the notebooks are stored online, you can edit them from your home, office, or anywhere else, as long as you have a browser and an Internet connection. You can share the notebooks you store on SkyDrive or an Office 365 team site (although you don't have to share notebooks to edit them with OneNote Web App).

TIP   You can sign up for a Microsoft Account at *https://signup.live.com*. After creating an account, you can log on to SkyDrive and access your files and OneNote Web App at *www.skydrive.live.com* through a web browser.

SEE ALSO   To learn how to create a notebook on SkyDrive, read "Creating a notebook on SkyDrive" on page 254. To learn how to create a folder on SkyDrive, read "Creating SkyDrive folders for storing notebooks" on page 252. To learn how to create and share notebooks on an Office 365 team site, read "Creating a Notebook in Office 365" on page 260.

Creating SkyDrive folders for storing notebooks

SkyDrive is an online storage space where you can create and edit OneNote notebooks, create and manage folders for storing notebooks, and invite other people to collaborate with you.

You can create a folder on SkyDrive for storing notebooks online (and storing other types of files if you want). By default, SkyDrive provides one folder for you: the Documents folder. You can create as many folders as you need to organize your work.

Create a SkyDrive folder for storing notebooks

1   Log on to SkyDrive at *www.skydrive.live.com* or, on the Start screen, click the SkyDrive tile.

(continued on next page)

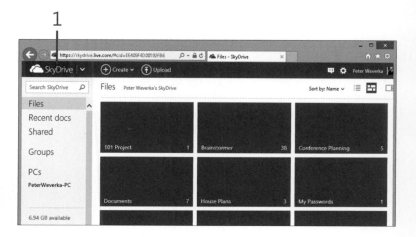

1

TIP   Use these techniques to manage folders in the SkyDrive window:

- **Viewing folders**   Click the Details View or Thumbnails View button (located in the upper-right corner of the SkyDrive window) to change your view of folders. To display a file's properties (the date it was created, last modified, size, and with whom it's shared), click the Show or Hide the Details Pane button.

- **Selecting folders**   In Thumbnails view, select the check box in the upper-right corner of the folder's tile; in Details view, select the folder's check box.

- **Deleting folders**   Select folder(s), click the Manage button, and then, on the drop-down list that appears, choose Delete. The contents of deleted folders land in the Recycle Bin in case you want to restore them. Click Recycle Bin in the SkyDrive pane to open the Recycle Bin and rescue a folder that you didn't mean to delete.

Create a SkyDrive folder for storing
notebooks *(continued)*

2 3

2 On the toolbar at the top of the SkyDrive window, click the Create button.

3 On the menu that appears, click Folder.

4 Enter a name.

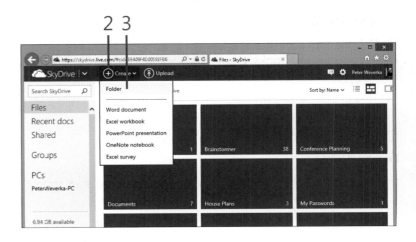

4

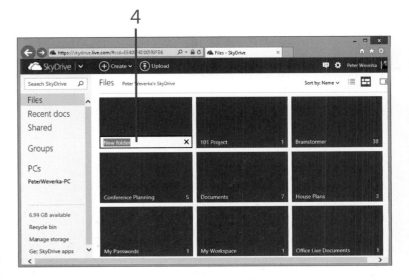

✓ **TIP** You can store 7 GB of data on SkyDrive (and purchase more space if you want). The SkyDrive window lists how many gigabytes of data are available for storage (look in the lower-left corner of the window).

Creating a notebook on SkyDrive

You can create a OneNote notebook starting in SkyDrive. After you create the notebook, it opens in OneNote Web App.

Create a notebook on SkyDrive

1 On SkyDrive, click to open the folder where you want to store the notebook.

2 On the toolbar at the top of the SkyDrive window, click the Create button.

3 On the menu that appears, click OneNote Notebook.

(continued on next page)

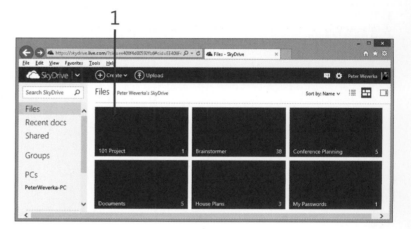

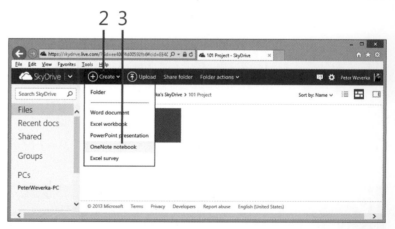

Create a notebook on SkyDrive *(continued)*

4 In the New Microsoft OneNote Notebook dialog box, enter a name.

5 Click Create.

The notebook opens in OneNote Web App.

6 Use the OneNote Web App tools to edit the notebook.

Changes you make are saved automatically.

7 Click SkyDrive to return to the SkyDrive window.

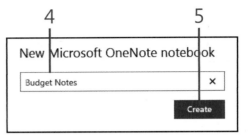

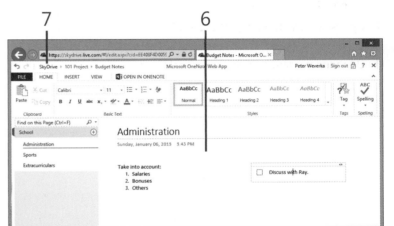

> **✓ TIP** Use these techniques to manage notebooks (and other files) in a SkyDrive folder:
>
> - **Selecting notebooks** In Thumbnails view, select the check box in the upper-right corner of the notebook's tile; in Details view, select the notebook's check box. You can select more than one notebook by selecting multiple check boxes.
>
> - **Deleting notebooks** Select the notebook, click Manage, and then, on the drop-down menu that appears, click Delete.
>
> - **Renaming notebooks** Select the notebook, click Manage, and then, on the drop-down menu that appears, click Rename and enter a name.
>
> - **Moving notebooks** Select the notebook, click Manage, and then, on the drop-down menu that appears, click Move To. Then, in the Selected Item Will Be Moved To dialog box, select a folder and click Move.

> **✓ TIP** To open an existing notebook in OneNote Web App, open the folder where the notebook is stored and click the notebook's tile (in Thumbnails view) or name (in Details view).

Opening a SkyDrive notebook in OneNote

When you want to do a task that you can do in OneNote 2013 but not in OneNote Web App, open your notebook in OneNote 2013. OneNote Web App even offers a button that you can click to open a notebook in OneNote.

Open a SkyDrive notebook in OneNote

1 Open the notebook in OneNote Web app.

2 On the ribbon, click Open In OneNote.

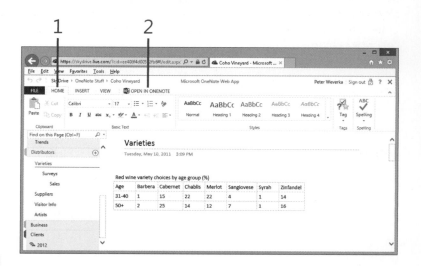

 TIP You can also open a notebook in OneNote by using these techniques:

- Click File and choose Open In OneNote.
- On the View tab, click Reading View. Then, click the Edit Notebook button and on the drop-down menu that appears, click Edit In Microsoft OneNote.

⚠ CAUTION If you installed OneNote App for Windows 8 from the Windows Store, clicking Open In OneNote might cause the notebook to open there. To change this, in Windows 8, Open the Control Panel, click Programs, click Default Programs, and then click Set Default Programs. Set OneNote (desktop) to the default for the protocol ONENOTE.

Inviting others to share a notebook on SkyDrive

Share a notebook with others so that they can work on it, too. Sharing is a great way to collaborate with other people and trade ideas about a project. If you share notebooks through SkyDrive, people who collaborate with you do not need to have OneNote 2013 or a Microsoft Account (unless you require it for security reasons).

The person who shares the notebook initially is called the *owner*. When sharing, the owner determines which of the following editing privileges *sharers* have:

- **Can view**   A sharer can view the notebook but not edit it.
- **Can edit**   A sharer can view and edit the notebook.

Before you share a notebook, make sure you have the email addresses of the people with whom you want to share it. You send invitations by email to share the notebook.

Invite others to share a SkyDrive notebook

1 On SkyDrive, select the notebook that you want to share.

2 On the toolbar, click Sharing.

(continued on next page)

> **TIP**   To find out the names of people with whom you share a notebook, select the notebook in SkyDrive and click the Show or Hide the Details Pane button. The Details pane lists sharers' names. You can change a sharer's edit/view status by clicking the Can View or Can Edit link and choosing Can View or Can Edit link on the drop-down menu. Click the Remove Permissions button in the Details pane to cease sharing a notebook with someone.

Invite others to share a SkyDrive
notebook *(continued)*

3 In the Send A Link dialog box, enter the email address of the sharer. If the sharer is a SkyDrive contact, you can simply type his name.

You can enter more than one address to share the notebook with multiple sharers. Just be sure to separate each email address with a comma.

4 Write a note to accompany the invitation. You can explain why you want to share the notebook and the project or topic the notebook covers.

5 Select the Recipient Can Edit check box to permit the sharer to edit as well as view the notebook.

6 Select the Require Everyone Who Accesses This To Sign In check box to require the sharer to have a Microsoft Account in order to view and edit the notebook.

7 Click Share. Emails are sent to the recipients you entered, with a link to the shared notebook.

3 4

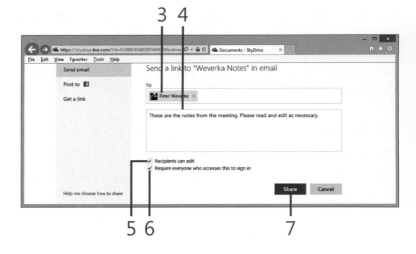

5 6   7

✓ **TIP** Click Shared in the SkyDrive pane to open the Files Shared With You window and see the names of folders and files that others have shared with you. You can open a folder or file from this window.

Finding out who made changes to a SkyDrive notebook

Any number of people can share a notebook on SkyDrive. What's more, they can write notes at the same time and make other changes. And some of them can be working in OneNote Web App and others in OneNote 2013 or OneNote Mobile.

When several people coauthor a notebook, how can you tell who made changes?

Find out who made changes to a SkyDrive notebook

1 In a notebook open on SkyDrive, on the ribbon, click the View tab.

2 Click the Show Authors button.

The name of each author appears next to each note or other item.

Creating a notebook in Office 365

Office 365 is a subscription service from Microsoft that provides various services (depending on your subscription level) such as cloud storage, email, shared calendars, instant messaging, online editing of Office documents (using Office Web App and/or streaming versions of the full programs known as Office on Demand), public website, and a SharePoint team site for document collaboration.

With an Office 365 subscription level that provides a team site, you can store files on that site and collaborate with others by using Office Web Application software, OneNote Web App included. To run OneNote Web App software with an Office 365 team site, you open your web browser, go to your Office 365 team site, and give commands through your browser to operate the software.

If you have Office 365 Home Premium, notebooks are stored on SkyDrive, not a team site, so you would go to SkyDrive to create and edit OneNote notebooks by using OneNote Web App instead of following the steps given here.

Create a notebook in Office 365

1 Go to the Home page of your Office 365 site.

2 Click the OneNote Icon.

(continued on next page)

Create a notebook in Office 365 (continued)

3 Enter a name for the notebook.

4 Click OK.

The notebook is opened in OneNote Web App.

TIP Notebooks you create on your Office 365 team site are available automatically for sharing (but only to people with whom you share the site). You don't need to choose an option to share notebooks with others.

TIP To open a notebook, on the main Office 365 team site page, click Shared Documents, and then click the notebook's name. Close the notebook by clicking File and clicking Close.

Index

Symbols

About the author

Peter Weverka is a veteran author of several dozen computer books about Microsoft Office software, including *Microsoft OneNote 2010 Plain & Simple*.

What do you think of this book?

We want to hear from you!
To participate in a brief online survey, please visit:

microsoft.com/learning/booksurvey

Tell us how well this book meets your needs—what works effectively, and what we can do better.
Your feedback will help us continually improve our books and learning resources for you.

Thank you in advance for your input!